W9-DFF-544

ADVANCES IN LIFELONG EDUCATION

CURRICULUM EVALUATION
FOR
LIFELONG EDUCATION

Developing Criteria and Procedures
for the Evaluation of School Curricula
in the Perspective of Lifelong Education:
A Multinational Study

CURRICULUM EVALUATION FOR LIFELONG EDUCATION

Developing Criteria and Procedures
for the Evaluation of School Curricula
in the Perspective of Lifelong Education:
A Multinational Study

Edited by

RODNEY SKAGER

University of California, Los Angeles

and

R.H. DAVE

International Institute for Education Planning, Paris

With contributions by

K.G. ROBINSON

Unesco Institute for Education, Hamburg

Published for the

UNESCO INSTITUTE FOR EDUCATION

by

PERGAMON PRESS

OXFORD · NEW YORK · TORONTO · SYDNEY · PARIS · FRANKFURT

U.K.   Pergamon Press Ltd., Headington Hill Hall,
                        Oxford OX3 0BW, England

U.S.A.   Pergamon Press Inc., Maxwell House, Fairview Park,
                        Elmsford, New York 10523, U.S.A.

CANADA   Pergamon of Canada Ltd., 75 The East Mall,
                        Toronto, Ontario, Canada

AUSTRALIA   Pergamon Press (Aust.) Pty. Ltd., 19a Boundary Street,
                        Rushcutters Bay, N.S.W. 2011, Australia

FRANCE   Pergamon Press SARL, 24 rue des Ecoles,
                        75240 Paris, Cedex 05, France

FEDERAL REPUBLIC   Pergamon Press GmbH, 6242 Kronberg/Taunus,
OF GERMANY   Pferdstrasse 1, Federal Republic of Germany

First edition 1977

Reprinted 1978

Library of Congress Cataloging in Publication Data
Skager, Rodney W   1932-
Curriculum evaluation for lifelong education.
(Advances in lifelong education; v. 2)
1. Adult education. I. Dave, R.H., joint author.
II. Robinson, Kenneth Girdwood, joint author.
III. Title. IV Series.
LC5219.S545 1976   374   77-8593
0 08 021816 4 (hardcover)
0 08 021817 2 (flexicover)

In order to make this volume available as economically and rapidly as possible the author's typescript has been reproduced in its original form. This method unfortunately has its typographical limitations but it is hoped that they in no way distract the reader.

Printed in Great Britain by William Clowes & Sons Limited, London, Beccles and Colchester

NOTES ON CONTRIBUTORS

SKAGER,   Rodney (United States). Is an Associate Professor in
the Graduate School of Education at the University of
California, Los Angeles. He has broad experience in
the field of educational evaluation and in the disciplines of measurement and educational research methods. For the past ten years Professor Skager has also
been associated with the Center for the Study of Evaluation at UCLA. Before joining the faculty of the
School he was a research psychologist with the Educational Testing Service in Princeton, New Jersey and
later with the America College Testing Program in
Iowa City, Iowa. While on academic leave during 1975-
1976 he served as Senior Educational Research Specialist at the Unesco Institute for Education in Hamburg.

DAVE,   Ravindra H. (India). Studied at universities of Bombay,
Gujerat and Chicago. In 1976 joined the International
Institute for Educational Planning (Paris), after com-
pleting four years as Technical Director at the Unesco
Institute for Education, Hamburg. His previous ex-
perience included the post of Dean of Educational De-
velopment, National Council of Educational Research
and Training, New Delhi; he directed the first Asian
Curriculum Research Project. His publications include
*Lifelong Education and School Curriculum; Reflections
on Lifelong Education and the School,* and *Studies in
Educational Evaluation and Assessment.*

ROBINSON, Kenneth G. (United Kingdom). Studied at Oxford and
London universities. Worked for fifteen years in
Singapore and Sarawak holding posts from teacher to
Dy. Director of Education, followed by seven years in
Cameroon as UNESCO specialist in planning and curri-
culum reform. Is now Head of Publications Unit at
Unesco Institute for Education, Hamburg. Publications
include contributions to *Die Musik in Geschichte und
Gegenwart* (Chinese music) and to *Chinese Science and
Civilization,* Vol.IV (acoustics), and also *English
Teaching in S.E. Asia.*

CONTENTS

CONTENTS

FOREWORD

For the last few years UNESCO has specially emphasised the
concept of lifelong education and used it whenever possible in
formulating its programs and policies. The Governing Board of
the Unesco Institute for Education took note of this growing
emphasis by directing the Institute to develop a long term research program aimed at the exploration and elaboration of the
concept of lifelong education, focussing primarily on education
at school level. While a great deal of work had already been
done, it was clear that the time had arrived for clarification
and systematization of the various conceptual features of lifelong education. It was equally evident that later work must
come to grips with the concrete implications of the concept, especially as related to the organization of schooling and to the
teaching and learning process. The present study is in many respects an initial step into the latter domain.

As the principles of lifelong education have implications
for virtually all types of society it is appropriate that this
first attempt to state and apply criteria for evaluating school
curricula according to these principles involves the cooperative
efforts of research teams from three countries. A multinational
effort provides a rich source of illustrative approaches to the
development of evaluative criteria and procedures, as was intended in the present study. Developing evaluative criteria and
procedures is an effective way to move from the conceptual to
the more concrete. Moreover, unless the capability exists for
evaluating contemporary curricula in terms of new criteria, it
is impossible to formulate rational policies for change. Evaluation is thus itself essential in bringing the principles of
lifelong education into operation.

The staff of the Unesco Institute for Education has been
indeed fortunate to have had a chance to work with members of
the three national teams cooperating in the research. The education ministries of the nations involved made this study possible
through their generous support of the work of these teams. Especially helpful in securing the cooperation at the national
level were Professor Masumori Hiratsuka, Director General of the
National Institute for Educational Research, in Japan, and Professor Sixten Marklund, Head of Division for Teacher Training
and Research and Development in Education, National Board of

ix

Education, in Sweden. We are particularly grateful for the contact we have had with the individuals who participated in one
or both of the two project workshops held at UIE: Professor
Kentaro Kihara, Professor Shigeo Masui and Dr. Eiichi Kajita
for Japan, Dr. Leon Topa, Dr. Costache Olareanu and Dr. Emilian
Dimitriu for Romania, Dr. Kurt Gestrelius and Dr. Lennart
Fredriksson for Sweden.

The Unesco Institute for Education is appreciative also
of the professional assistance provided by UNESCO's *Division of
Structures, Content, Methods and of Lifelong Education* in the
planning and concluding stages of the project, as well as for
the financial contribution which they have made.

It is important to clarify each author's contribution to
this report which was in every sense a collaborative effort,
although there was a definite division of responsibility among
authors. Dr. Dave conceived the study itself, developed its design, prepared other intermediate documents and reports used as
resource materials for the final report, and coordinated the
national and international phases of the work. He also planned,
prepared materials for, and conducted the initial and final
meetings of the participants, prepared an outline for the final
report and contributed a number of useful suggestions and comments on the draft of this document. The preparation of the
final report was carried out by Professor Rodney Skager after
Dr. Dave left the Unesco Institute. Professor Skager took part
in the final meeting of the participants with primary responsibility for organizing the discussion on empirical research. The
report was written by him virtually in its entirety. Mr. K.G.
Robinson coordinated the editing and revision of the combined
list of evaluative criteria and wrote the section dealing with
the history of lifelong education. Appendices 2, 3, 4, and 5
were taken from project documents prepared by Dr. Dave.

In addition to presenting conceptual material on curriculum and evaluation, the resulting document integrates and syn-
thesizes the procedures as well as the results of the national
research studies. The collaborative efforts of the individuals
mentioned above have produced a document that significantly en-
larges on the excellent work of the three national teams.

M. Dino Carelli

Director

CHAPTER 1

LIFELONG EDUCATION AND
EVALUATION OF SCHOOL CURRICULA

Purpose of Report

This report describes the procedures, results, and implications of a two year effort by teams from three nations to develop and utilize a set of criteria for evaluating school curricula. The criteria were derived from the principles of lifelong education and the national teams worked in cooperation
with the Unesco Institute for Education. The purposes of this
report are to:

1) describe the process by which the criteria were
   developed at the national level and later combined
   into a common, multi-national set;

2) present the resulting multi-national criteria with
   suggestions as to how further specification and
   implementation might proceed;

3) summarize and compare the strategies used by the
   teams in the evaluation of their own curricula
   according to the national criteria, and

4) summarize and compare the implications for curriculum improvement drawn by the national teams.

The research summarized in this report is at best an early step toward the concretization of the principles of lifelong
education. It seeks to isolate the salient characteristics of a
curriculum which incorporates the principles of lifelong education as well as to describe several procedures for applying the
resulting criteria to written and operational curricula. This
report draws heavily on the work of cooperating teams from
Japan, Romania, and Sweden who, after an initial joint planning
conference, developed their own versions of the lifelong educa-

1

tion criteria and in various ways applied those criteria to their own national curricula (1).

The writers will not attempt to draw comparisons between curricula of the three participating nations in terms of how closely each corresponds to the principles of lifelong education. This was never the intent of the study. Each team developed its own, partly unique, set of evaluative criteria and then proceeded to apply those criteria in different ways and, in most cases, to different aspects of their own national curricula. The comparisons in this report reflect this diversity by stressing differences in the procedures by which the national criteria were developed and in the manner in which each national team went about studying its own curriculum. The intention is to present alternatives and possibilities that may be of use in other nations rather than to prescribe a particular way of going about the evaluation of school curricula. Even where common ground has been deliberately established, as in the list of combined criteria, our aim is to sketch in starting points that can be modified and extended by others working in the field.

Before describing the research itself, the development of the idea of lifelong education should be reviewed. The evaluative criteria discussed in Chapter 4 of this report represent the most detailed specification to date of the various educational principles subsumed under lifelong education. Here we will emphasize the historical content out of which lifelong education has developed and the functions it is seen as fulfilling.

Origins of Lifelong Education

The idea of lifelong education seems to have its earliest origins in the field of adult education. Jessup (1969) quotes the 1919 Report of the Adult Education Committee of the Ministry of Reconstruction:

"The economic recovery of the nation, the sound exercise of the new spirit of assertion among the rank and file, the proper use of their responsibilities by millions of new voters, all alike depend on there being a far wider body of intelligent public opinion after the war than there was before, and such a public opinion can only be created gradually by a long,

thorough, universal process of education continued
into and throughout the life of the adult." (p.18).

The committee concluded that adult education was a necessity to
the British nation and as a result should be both universal and
"lifelong".

The idea that adult education should be permanent eventually took root. We may note the founding of the first Centre
for Continuing Education at the University of Minnesota in 1934.
There followed a period in which education of the future was
thought of as *continuing*, perhaps intermittently, from a period
of formal schooling; *continuous* in which life is not punctuated
by refresher courses, but regarded as a continuous process of
learning; and *permanent*, the term still used in France, which
suggests that traditional school level education is insufficient for the needs of individuals who will spend a lifetime in
a changing world and that, as a result, means must be made
available for making education a continuous, lifetime process.

The origin of the term itself is uncertain, but it was
used by UNESCO (1962) in the *Draft Programme and Budget for
1963-1964* as follows:

"Continuing Education. This section deals with
lifelong education for adults " (p.198).

Six years later the idea had matured. The UNESCO (1968)
Draft Programme and Budget for 1969-1970 reveals a significant
elaboration of the concept:

"Lifelong education was long regarded in certain
circles as a new term for adult education designed to emphasize the continuity of the latter.
This concept, however, has gradually become
broader and has assumed new dimensions. It is
being ever more frequently used to designate all
the ideas and activities whose aim is to provide
a coherent and systematic view of the educational
process as a whole, in order to meet more adequately the educational needs of individuals and
groups. It is now recognized, for instance, that
the education of children should be considered
in a new light and should be radically reorganized seeing that the idea that it comes to an
end with examinations and diplomas, has been
abandoned in favour of the view that it can and

should continue throughout life. Conversely, the
adult's capacity for study, training, advanced
training and intellectual, cultural and moral
progress in general depends directly on the
scope, nature and quality of the education he
has received during his childhood and adoles-
cence " (p.20).

Still, one cannot have "a coherent and systematic view of
the educational process as a whole" if one fails to take into
account the vital years between birth and the beginning of
formal education. The document just quoted does stress the need
for a fundamental organization of the education of children in
the belief that the adult's capacity for "advanced training and
intellectual, cultural and moral progress" is contingent on
such reorganization.

The Need for Lifelong Education

Let us now consider why lifelong education seems relevant
to the times, and then return to it once more as a concept,
though in reality it is not a unitary concept but an organized
set of principles and aspirations.

Lifelong education is now receiving increasing worldwide
interest. Faure et al. (1972) cite developments in many nations as illustrations of the 21 principles embodied in the report. Perhaps the most significant reason for this interest is
the speed of contemporary social and technological change. For-
merly each generation grew up into a world that was remarkably
constant within a person's lifetime. This is no longer true. In
some cases ordinary people are aware of changes in the world
they live in, as when, for example, their village is swallowed
up in a growing metropolis, though they may not be aware of the
causes. In others they may not be aware of what is happening
even as a result of their own actions - as when, for example,
they contribute to the deterioration of the environment or the
exhaustion of raw materials. But frequently individuals, whether in the professions or in factories, are made brutally aware
that unless they re-educate themselves they will be put out of
business. Because the problems facing mankind are now so complex and develop so rapidly, new roles and forms of education
are required. This can no longer be encompassed in a few years
of formal schooling. It must be a process continuing all
through life from the earliest till the latest years.

Faure et al (1972) stress the urgency of the human situation. If school learning is insufficient, post-school supple-
ments must be devised quickly. But this is only an emergency
measure. More important is the reorganization of formal schooling through its interaction with a larger, continuous educational network. Carried to its logical conclusion, this implies the
reorganization of society itself, especially in the sense of
flexibility in the means, source, and time of learning. In the
distant future the normal pattern of life may be one of alter-
nating periods of work or action, followed by periods of education or re-education, together with a heightened process of
learning by doing continued throughout active life.

The Significance of Lifelong Education

This new vision of society is expressed in the notion of
"the learning society". Faure et al. (1972) maintain:

> "Education from now on can no longer be defined in
> relation to a fixed content which has to be assi-
> milated, but must be conceived of as a process in
> the human being ..." (p.143).

A learning society

> "implies that every citizen should have the means
> of learning, training and cultivating himself,
> freely available to him, under all circumstances
> ..." (p.163).

This vision has vast implications in the use of resources and
the nature of society itself.

This view of the learning society is very much the view
of highly industrialized countries which have the means for
enabling individuals to train and cultivate themselves. However, even in such countries full implementation of the principles of lifelong education would require an extensive dis-
persal of educational resources throughout the society. If opportunity to learn does not exist, motivation for such learning on the part of individuals and groups would have no outlet.
Elvin (1975) has commented on the economic and social resources
that would have to be committed to the provision of full opportunity under lifelong education.

Lifelong education has a different function when looked
at from the point of view of countries in less advanced stages

of development. For them the cost of education may be a key
factor. It may be necessary to reduce the period of formal
school-level education, because the state has not the means to
give everyone a prolonged education in school. There is no
choice, then, but to continue education in other ways after
children have left school. In some countries continuing education in the form of political discussion, on-the-job training,
regular refresher courses, cadre school training and so on are
built into the system. This is done, however, not primarily in
order that individuals may cultivate themselves, but in order
to contribute to the larger society by helping the individual
to become a more productive member of a team.

It is well to realize from the start that lifelong education is concerned with liberty, with individuals, with institutions and with power, and can scarcely fail to be a matter of
supreme importance during the coming century. It is not surprising, therefore, that lifelong education was proposed by
UNESCO (1972) as

> "the master concept for educational policies in the
> years to come for the developed and developing
> countries". (p.182).

Lifelong Education Described

What then is lifelong education? The description evolved
by UNESCO in 1968 for the purposes of a work plan in the *Draft
Programme and Budget for 1969-1970* quoted above gives an idea
of the breadth of concern implied by lifelong education. One
may also cite Dave (1975):

> "Lifelong education is a comprehensive concept
> which includes formal, non-formal and informal
> learning extended throughout the life-span of
> an individual to attain the fullest possible de-
> velopment in personal, social and professional
> life. It seeks to view education in its totality
> and includes learning that occurs in the home,
> school, community, and workplace, and through
> mass media and other situations and structures
> for acquiring and enhancing enlightenment. In
> this context the concept of lifelong education
> provides a new perspective to all educational
> goals, activities and structures, emphasizing
> the all-round development of the individual

over the whole life-span. Lifelong education is
not just preparation for life, it is an integral
part of life. Learning and living are closely
intertwined, each enriching the other. Thus, lifelong education becomes a continuous quest for a
higher and better quality of life " (p.42).

Although lifelong education is perhaps best described as
an inclusive set of educational principles, Dave refers to it
as a concept in the above definition. Lifelong education is a
concept in one sense. It incorporates a comprehensive view of
the role of education in the lives of individuals as well as in
the broader society. At its core, the concept holds education
as the primary tool by which individuals and their societies
can adapt to the rapidly accelerating pace of change in the
modern world. It stresses individual and collective fulfillment
through continuing personal growth. Its view of society is that
of a cooperative system whose function is one of providing the
means for such personal growth by distributing educational alternatives throughout the social structures so as to be available to all individuals at virtually any time in their lives.

Lifelong education does not advocate de-schooling. Illich
(1975), for example, maintains:

"Being merely schooling in another guise, a policy
of lifelong education can never be anything but a
trap for attempts at de-schooling society."

In spite of Illich's concerns, proponents of lifelong education
do place great stress on the development of a vast array of separate, but coordinated educational alternatives, including
formal alternatives. The development of independence and autonomy in learners is also highly valued. Certainly much of the
lifelong education literature finds fault with the traditional
school along lines that are really quite similar to those drawn
by both the de-schoolers and the parallel reformist movement
that would retain the school as an institution, though one that
has been subjected to extensive reform. In this regard there is
very broad agreement among a variety of commentators that the
ambience of traditional schools is antithetical to the development and maintenance of independent thinking, autonomy, and internalized motivation for learning. Biggs (1973) suggests that
the "hidden" curriculum of the school often forces pupils to
depend on authorities in a way that denies them the opportunity
to learn how to diagnose personal needs, select modes of learning, and evaluate their own progress toward a goal. Likewise,

Cropley (1976) notes that the overt curriculum is criticized for over-emphasizing factual learning at the expense of the development of generalized, problem-solving skills.

Under lifelong education the school would still have a central role, although its main function would shift from granting "an education" in the terminal sense to one of preparing learners to continue their education by a variety of means, formal and informal, including self-study. Fostering motivation for later learning is seen as a vital function of the school. This view of the function of the school reflects the basic nature of lifelong education as a concept. It is concerned with fostering voluntary participation in an educational process that is lifelong, rather than one that is circumscribed within a phase of development merely preparatory to life. Likewise, it views education in its totality within human society instead of equating it with schooling. It seeks the coordination and integration as educational entities of the home, the mass media, other non-formal educational delivery systems, and most importantly the self.

Thinking on lifelong education has been organized and interpreted conceptually. The report of the Faure Committee (1972) proposes 21 guiding principles for the implementation of lifelong education. Dave (1975) generated a set of *concept characteristics* which define what lifelong education represents in a qualitative sense. These concept characteristics have been reproduced in Appendix 2. While Dave's complete list contains 20 characteristics, a set of 8 summary principles was derived for the project and these can be briefly defined here:

1) *Totality*, or viewing education in all its forms and manifestations;

2) *Integration*, or coordination of educational options available at any given point in time in the lives of individuals as well as throughout the total life-span;

3) *Flexibility*, or variation and diversity of educational content, modes of learning, and time of learning;

4) *Democratization*, or universalism in access to educational opportunity for all members of a society;

5) *Opportunity and Motivation*, comprising societal and personal prerequisites for the development of lifelong education;

6) *Educability*, or the central goal of lifelong education in the development of the individual, defined by Dave (1975) as a wider competence than "learning to learn" that includes "... skills of learning and sharing enlightenment, skills in self-evaluation and cooperative assessment, and above all, readiness to change and improve on the basis of learning, sharing and evaluation" (p.50).

7) *Operational modality*, or the recognition that education can proceed through formal, non-formal and informal channels and that the quality of learning is defined in its own terms rather than in terms of the means by which it was acquired, and

8) *Quality of Life and Learning*, or the recognition that the central societal function of education is that of enhancing the human experience.

The eight clusters constitute the starting point for the development of the curriculum evaluative criteria of the present report. The procedures followed and the criteria that resulted are the subject matter of Chapter 4.

There has been discussion as to whether one does best to speak of *lifelong education* or *lifelong learning*. In the present report the writers of the Swedish national report took the following position:

"In this report we often use the term 'lifelong learning' and not 'lifelong education'. This is because we think the word learning suggests the individual's own activity in connection with learning. Behind this lies the educational hypothesis: 'The individual himself is the only person who can be active in such a way that learning takes place...' " (p.11).

Certainly people do learn throughout their lives. But deliberate efforts to improve the direction and quality of such learning are necessary as well. Such efforts are implied by the term "lifelong education". Our specific concern here is with those aspects of education that are subsumed under the concept of curriculum. The term "lifelong education" is therefore used more frequently in the context of this report, although "lifelong learning" is relevant in other contexts.

The Practice of Lifelong Education

How then is lifelong education to be put into practice? Implementation involves a fundamental change in attitudes, and until this is accomplished little progress is likely to be made. Attitudes are changed in many ways, such as by the example of others and by discussion and reading. The publication of books and reports on lifelong education is a first necessity, for they will provoke discussion and stimulate example.

It is also necessary that lifelong education should be available, that the means to it should be within reach of those who wish for it. Opportunity, facilities and funds are more within the gift of institutions than the grasp of individuals. Opportunities for the continuing of education can be made by the reorganization of the working day and the working year, and are likely to increase as automation increases leisure. Facilities, including equipment for self-learning as well as teachers and classrooms of traditional type adopted for a new set of needs, are required. Resources for the support of continuing education are obviously needed, but as education already in most countries claims a very large share of a nation's budget, this will perhaps be a matter of reallocating the funds already made available for education rather than increasing the share of the whole. Realization of the principles of lifelong education on an extensive scale is thus as much dependent on changes in a society as it is dependent on changes in the attitudes and values of individuals and groups in that society. Significant transformations in the ways in which resources are allocated as well as an opening up of a wide variety of avenues of opportunity and access would be required in most if not all contemporary societies.

If lifelong education is to be made a reality in the near future, the curriculum of schools cannot be neglected. This need to reform school curricula can scarcely be exaggerated, for in most societies it is in school that children are or can be equipped with the means of continuing their education after they have left school. If the school fails so to equip them

their chances of successfully continuing their education there-
after are correspondingly reduced. Schools can become the
spring-board for implementing lifelong education.

Reforming School Curricula

The first step towards reconstruction of curricula must
therefore be to evaluate existing curricula, bearing clearly in
mind that it is the curriculum in its widest sense which equips
or fails to equip children to educate themselves throughout
their lives. By curriculum in its widest sense we mean not only
the traditional curriculum of school subjects, but the school's
latent curriculum, deriving from the pressures of school life,
its teaching methods, the interests and attitudes it induces
and so on. There is also in a real sense an out-of-school curriculum based on formal and informal education derived from the
home, the peer group, the media, and the culture at large. This
subject will be taken up in Chapter 3.

School curricula must be evaluated in order to identify
their strengths and weaknesses. The results of such evaluations
would be vital starting points in elaborating programmes of improvement that are sufficiently specific and realistic to offer
genuine hopes of success. The need for specificity and realism
is great. Theory is not enough. Concrete application is called
for. As Lengrand (1970) points out:

"Lifelong education is still at the conceptual
stage. As with other principles such as freedom,
justice and equality, it will doubtless retain
indefinitely that certain distance in relation
to concrete achievements which is in the nature
of concepts. If, however, the distance is too
great, ... scepticism will be aroused. The accu-
sations of vagueness, formlessness and imprecision which are often aimed at this concept are
not devoid of reason. If a notion is to emerge
from limbo and to appear in its true light, it
is essential that it should be reflected in
facts and actions from which it can draw strength.
For as long as analyses of lifelong education
are not backed by a series of references to situations, structures, programmes, in brief, to
all that is so aptly called the 'concrete', so
long will it be difficult to win mass support

for theses of which the foundations have so far
been largely theoretical " (p.98).

The work described in this report is timely in the light
of the needs just expressed. If the first step towards making
lifelong education a concrete reality is reform of school curricula, this report, we believe, will be of help to those responsible for the task. It is after all based on actual curriculum evaluation studies conducted in three countries. The next
chapter will describe how this project has been carried out.

NOTES

1. Information about the national reports is given in
   Appendix 1.

REFERENCES

Biggs, J.B. "Content and Process". *Australian Journal
of Education*, 17, 1973, pp.225-238.

Cropley, A. "Some Psychological Reflections on Lifelong Education". In Dave, R.H. (ed.) *Foundations of
Lifelong Education*. Oxford: Pergamon Press, 1976.

Dave, R.H. *Lifelong Education and School Curriculum*.
UIE Monograph 1. Hamburg: Unesco Institute for Education, 1973.

Dave, R.H. *Reflections on Lifelong Education and the
School*. UIE Monograph 3. Hamburg: Unesco Institute
for Education, 1975.

Elvin, L. "Learning to Be ..." *Education News*, 15,
No. 1, 1975, pp.24-29.

Faure, E. et al. *Learning to Be: The World of Education Today and Tomorrow*. Paris: UNESCO; London:
Harrup, 1972.

Illich, I. and Verne, E. "Le Piège de l'Ecole à la Vie".
Le Monde de l'Education, Janvier 1975.

Jessup, F.W. *Lifelong Learning: A Symposium on Continuing Education*. Oxford: Pergamon Press, 1969.

Lengrand, P. *Introduction to Lifelong Education*. Paris:
    UNESCO, 1970.

UNESCO. *Draft Programme and Budget for 1963-1964*.
    Paris: UNESCO, 1962.

UNESCO. *Draft Programme and Budget for 1969-1970*.
    Paris: UNESCO, 1968.

CHAPTER 2

PLANS AND PROCEDURES OF THE STUDY

Since the present research was designed to identify and try out alternative criteria and evalution procedures, a co-operative multinational approach appeared to offer significant advantages over the study of totally independent national efforts or intensive case studies within single countries. In the multinational approach adopted here the participating teams first met together at the Unesco Institute for Education, Hamburg, in order to work out an initial framework and a preliminary list of criteria for lifelong education. This provided a common terminology and set of understandings from which the national teams could proceed to develop evaluative criteria and procedures suitable to their own situations. This chapter will provide an overview of the procedural and organizational aspects of the study.

Phases of the Study

Although a detailed list of stages will be given at the end of the chapter, the study can be seen as a project with five basic phases:

1) Previous conceptual work on lifelong education was used to prepare an overall project design as well as a set of written materials to be distributed to members of the cooperating national teams.

2) An initial planning workshop was held at the UIE with two members from each of the national teams and participating UIE research staff.

3) National phases of the study were undertaken in the 22 months that elapsed between the initial and final workshops. During this period

national teams prepared concrete research designs at the national level, revised and extended the initial criterion list for lifelong
education to suit the national context, conducted the evaluation studies and wrote final
reports.

4) When the national reports had been completed
and their English language versions distributed, participants again convened at UIE to
present and discuss national procedures and
findings and to develop a combined or multinational criterion list compatible with the
national lists. Considerable time was devoted
in this meeting to comparing the national
studies in order to facilitate their later
synthesis in the present report.

5) During the months following the final workshop this report was written and its initial
draft distributed to the national teams for
comments. The latter were incorporated into
the final version.

The National Teams

The Swedish team operated from a different type of institutional base than did the other teams and with fewer personnel.
The two individuals responsible for the Swedish report were located in a university rather than a national educational research agency, specifically the Department of Educational and
Psychological Research of the School of Education, University
of Malmö. Their work was sponsored by the Swedish Board of Education. The Japanese and Romanian teams were located, respectively, in the National Institute for Educational Research,
Tokyo, and the Institute of Pedagogical and Psychological Research, Bucharest. Considerably larger personnel resources were
devoted to the project in the latter two countries, with eleven
individuals listed as having at least part time participation
for Japan and nine for Romania.

The difference in personnel complements was reflected in
the fact that only one empirical study, an elaborate content
analysis of the curriculum, was conducted by the members of the
Swedish team. However, the considerable array of existing empirical research studies on Swedish education was extensively

utilized by the Swedes. Their work was thus greatly extended through reference to available research on the national curriculum.

Observations on the National Curricula

Probably the most salient characteristic of the educational systems of the three participating countries is the fact that each is organized under a centralized educational authority with all schools deriving their instructional programs from a national written curriculum. Proposals for reform in the curriculum apply to the nation as a whole in all three cases. Likewise, in all three countries the school is the primary medium of delivery for education. Some basic features of the three national curricula are provided in Table 2.1 (see pp.17-18).

Japan

The Japanese curriculum incorporates nine years of compulsory schooling, split into six years of primary school and three years of lower secondary. While upper secondary is not compulsory, 90% or more of the age cohort now enter at this level. Locally developed (prefecture level) achievement tests are utilized for admissions purposes at the upper secondary level. Contemporary trends toward high utilization of upper secondary schools by a much more academically heterogeneous student population than was the case in the past have necessitated reforms in the total curriculum, and the Curriculum Reform Commission has been working hard for that purpose since November, 1973. There has also been an increase in attendance at private schools, partly as preparation for admission to selective schools perceived by the public as offering a more valuable diploma. About 60% of the upper secondary level learners are enrolled in general or academic curricula, with the remaining 40% in various vocational streams. Learners graduating from the latter can gain admission to universities, but are handicapped by the entrance examination which is based on several subjects in the category of General Education. Serious consideration is also given at present to the resolution of this problem. Generally, the situation in Japan appears to be one of greatly increased utilization of educational opportunity, both public and private, with concomitantly vigorous competition for the most favoured places.

TABLE 2.1

A COMPARISON OF FEATURES OF THE JAPANESE,
ROMANIAN AND SWEDISH NATIONAL CURRICULA

CURRICULUM	JAPAN
Age for starting school	6
Years of schooling normally taken	12
Years of compulsory schooling	9
Stages and grades	1- 6: Elementary school 7- 9: Lower secondary school 10-12: Upper secondary school
Stage- and level-wise objectives	Overall statement only in a law; but objectives stated for each stage
Subject-wise objectives	Statement of objectives at each level and grade
Curriculum plan	By order of the Ministry of Education a common curriculum plan for the entire country; however, individual teachers still have considerable freedom to devise their own curriculum plan.

TABLE 2.1 cont.

ROMANIA	SWEDEN
6	7
12	11-13
10	9
1- 4: Primary school 5- 8: Gymnasium 9-12: Lycée (two years compulsory)	1- 6: Primary school 7- 9: Lower secondary school 10-11/ Secondary school 13: 2-4 years
General statement for all levels and also for each grade	Objectives for each primary year. Secondary objectives are similar to primary
Statement of objectives at each level (but not at grades)	Statement of objectives at each level and grade
Documents describe curriculum for primary and secondary levels. Syllabi exist for subjects which are subdivided in grades. These are uniform for the whole country.	National statement of philosophy or policy of plan. At primary level a number of books provide these plans for each subject at each level. At secondary level a nationally distributed booklet for each grade detailing plan for each subject.

Romania

The Romanian system is in the process of extending the period of compulsory schooling from 8 to 10 years toward an eventual goal of 12 years by the year 1990. The schools are organized on the three tiered system of primary (grades 1 - 4), lower secondary (grades 6 - 8), and upper secondary (grades 9 - 12). The curriculum itself places a great deal of stress on the acquisition of scientific knowledge, on the development of conceptual structures for interpreting natural and social phenomena scientifically, and on the implementation of scientific knowledge. Equally important is the integration of technical and productive work activities into the curriculum through work experience programmes. The guiding ideal is one of bringing intellectual and physical work close together in order to facilitate integration of graduates into productive work-roles.

Sweden

Sweden has 9 year compulsory or basic school, also divided into three levels corresponding to primary (grades 1 - 3), middle (grades 4 - 6), and lower secondary (grades 7 - 9). Students usually start school in their seventh year following (for the great majority) at least one year of voluntary attendance at a pre-school. Over 80% of students leaving the lower secondary voluntarily continue in upper secondary school in 2 to 4 year programmes. This last segment of schooling is split between theoretical and practical streams. While the former is oriented to admission to higher education, it is possible to move from the practical to the academic by utilizing agencies which provide compensatory educational programmes. But not many learners are willing to make this kind of programme switch.

Operational Schema of the Project

The Flow Chart (Fig. 2.1, p. 20) is taken in slightly modified form from the document summarizing the deliberations of the initial planning workshop. It reveals the project to be concerned with two major domains of *lifelong education* and *school curriculum*. The sequence shows that the project begins with the study of the implications of lifelong education yielding a set of "concept characteristics" (Appendix 2) from which were derived a set of implications for the school curriculum. The latter in turn provide the basis for the development of concrete criteria for evaluating curricula according to the principles of lifelong education.

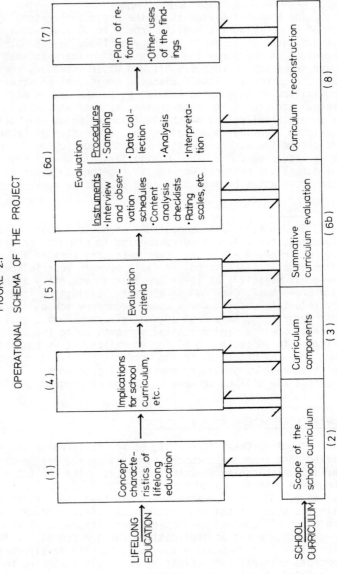

FIGURE 2.1

OPERATIONAL SCHEMA OF THE PROJECT

A parallel activity in the second or curriculum domain involves first defining the actual scope of the school curriculum and in turn analyzing that curriculum into components which will ultimately be the foci of various aspects of curriculum evaluation. There are a series of sequential and simultaneous interactions between the two domains, as shown by the arrows on the flow chart. For example, the evaluation criteria evolve in reference to various curriculum components such as objectives, content, methods of teaching and learning, and other components to be defined in the next chapter. Once developed, the criteria are adapted to particular curriculum components by selecting appropriate instruments, sampling strategies, procedures of data collection, and the like. This reflects, for example, the fact that one would use different instruments and strategies for evaluating curriculum objectives than would be used in the evaluation of the teaching/learning process. In turn, evaluation instruments and procedures are often revised on the basis of what has been learned from an actual evaluation study, as the double arrows between 6a and 6b suggest.

The ultimate goal of the two interacting domains of activity is to identify specific steps for improving a curriculum through renovation and reform. An effective evaluation should constitute the basis for a plan of reform by revealing where changes are needed and for what purposes they are needed. The operational schema in the flow chart thus summarizes in abstract form the series of independent and at the same time integrated research steps which underlie the present project.

Overview of Project Stages

Up to this point this report has summarized the historical context from which lifelong education had devolved up to the time this project began and described the project's background and organizational structure. Next we will define the concepts of curriculum, curriculum component, and curriculum evaluation. Before proceeding with this task it seems useful to wind up the present one by surveying the major steps of the project in order to relate them to the material which follows. The project, then, can be divided into ten sequential stages:

1) Preparation of overall project design for cooperative, multinational study.

2) Preparation of materials for initial multinational conference including concept character-

istics of lifelong education which served as
starting point for development of evaluative
criteria.

3) Convening of first international workshop,
February 18-28, 1974, to (a) develop initial
list of evaluative criteria from concept
characteristics and (b) arrive at initial research and development designs for the national studies.

4) Revision of criteria and research designs by
national teams working in own countries
(Chapter 4).

5) Application of criteria to written curricula
by national teams (Chapter 5).

6) Application by national teams of criteria to
operational curriculum by (a) survey of pertinent literature and (b) empirical studies
of students, parents, and teachers, etc.
(Chapter 5).

7) Preparation of national reports and submission
for review by other national teams and UIE
staff.

8) Convening of second multinational workshop
December 1-12, 1975, to (a) present national
reports, (b) construct summaries of comparable national procedures and findings for input to final report, (Chapters 4 and 5), and
(c) generate new list of combined criteria
from separate national lists (Chapter 4).

9) Revision and editing of combined criteria by
UIE staff (Appendix 5).

10) Preparation of final report by UIE.

If one considers that the first stage occurred in 1973 and
the last in the Spring of 1976, then the full project can be
seen to have stretched over a period of nearly three years.
However, the data collection phase extended over approximately
one school year. The latter could certainly be a much longer
phase in the case of other projects collecting longitudinal or
other data over longer time periods.

CHAPTER 3

SCHOOL CURRICULUM AND ITS EVALUATION

Defining Curriculum

The term "curriculum" is used at various levels of inclusiveness in educational discourse. Sometimes it refers only
to a set of guidelines as to the content of instruction, in
other cases to curriculum plans which may be quite detailed in
the sense of incorporating specifications as to instructional
objectives, *content*, and *methods*. (We will see shortly that
these basic components of instruction can be further differentiated.) But written plans and guidelines, no matter how detailed, represent a relatively restricted concept of the curriculum.

Separating content and method may be criticized as reflecting an artificial distinction that does not correspond to
the realities of the teaching/learning process. Educational
content and educational method doubtless interact in complex
ways. It can be argued that the manner in which something is
learned is in itself a part of content.

> "It is, in general, impossible to distinguish
> between the method and the content of education.
> Indeed, often processes should become the con-
> tent of education." (1)

Modes of learning can themselves be defined as learning goals
at the same time that they are processes. But distinguishing
between content and method is still useful in the development
of curricula and the design of evaluations.

A definition of curriculum that incorporates only formal
plans and guidelines is too restrictive from the perspective
of evaluation. Formal plans may have only a tenuous and indirect influence on the experience of learners in the classroom.

Curriculum is thus often thought of in much broader terms. In this sense the "real" curriculum, the curriculum actually experienced by the learner, incorporates everything, planned and unplanned, that has any significant bearing on what is learned. Payne (1974), in the introduction to a widely used text on curriculum evaluation, articulates this point of view:

> "However one ultimately defines curriculum, one must accept that it includes everything that directs and stimulates student experience and learning. For the most part, primary focus is on the educators' systematic and intentional efforts. Yet significant unplanned results do occur " (p.6).

Payne's definition of curriculum is consistent with the one adopted for this project. Working documents used at the initial meeting of project participants defined school curriculum as,

> "... *all goal directed educational activities that are generated by the school whether they take place in the institution or outside of it*".

This includes a "latent" or "hidden" curriculum that is not incorporated in the curriculum plan and that often may be unintentional in the sense of being unplanned.

Although the definition does not explicitly say so, we also recognize that there is a pervasive non-school curriculum operating in home and community that is assigned an explicit role under the framework of lifelong education. This is apparent, for example, in Dave (1975):

> "The skills and attitudes implicit in educability and self-directed learning will not be confined to school-based learning only, but will automatically be extended to the home-based and community-based situations of learning and sharing. For this, horizontal integration and vertical articulation of varied contents and means of learning will have to be ascertained. In order to take care of all these factors it will be essential to consider an entire "curricular spectrum" that encompasses all learning arrangements and situations along the dimensions of time and space " (p.51).

The importance of this wider curriculum operating outside of the school was stressed in material made available to participants in the present project. Recognition of the influence of a wider curricular spectrum will be apparent in some of the national research activities.

Finally, the concept of lifelong education introduces a new facet to curriculum in its emphasis on self-directed learning. As learners develop the independence and autonomy required for taking over responsibility for guiding their own learning activities, they must, implicitly or explicitly, begin to define their own curriculum. The broader concept of curriculum, ranging from an *individual* curriculum to that of the school, the community, the home, and some larger entity such as a nation or national region is as yet relatively inexplored.

Components of the Curriculum

It has been suggested already that curricula can be divided into components that are more specific than the commonly distinguished goals, content and methods. All curriculum components are potentially interactive. For example, the student's liking of a particular method of instruction may influence his response to the particular instructional content taught under that method. In the present study six components were initially formulated: Objectives, Curriculum Plan, Teaching Methods and Learning Activities, Learning Materials, Evaluation Procedures, and Curriculum Implementation.

1) *Objectives*: Statements about what the curriculum should accomplish may be made at many levels of inclusiveness, such as at the national level, for the entire school stage, for different grade levels of schooling or for different subject matter areas. The process through which objectives are developed is perhaps just as significant as the objectives themselves and is therefore an appropriate concern in the evaluation of this component of the curriculum.

2) *Curriculum Plan*: The curriculum plan is a formal design for implementing the objectives. It is usually thought of as incorporating two important facets, the first defining curriculum content and the second specifying desired

teaching/learning *processes*. The curriculum
plan is usually a written document that has
emerged from a complex interactive process.

3) *Teaching Methods and Learning Activities*: The
manner in which teaching and learning is finally carried out represents the real implementation of the objectives of the curriculum
as mediated by the curriculum plan. It is ob-
vious that discrepancies can arise between
educational objectives themselves, the plans
derived from those objectives, and the real
events that occur during the learning process.

4) *Learning Materials*: The materials utilized in
the learning process include textbooks and
exercise materials as well as a variety of
other aids such as libraries, audio-visual
centres and community learning resources such
as museums and exhibitions.

5) *Evaluation Procedures*: Evaluation refers here
primarily to pupil assessment, either formal
or informal. Evaluation at the level of the
learner has been analyzed in considerable detail by Skager (1977). It serves several functions in the teaching/learning process and
may be conducted by learners themselves, by
teachers, or by outside authorities.

6) *Curriculum Implementation*: This last major
component focusses on the manner in which curriculum change is introduced. It encompasses
the planning and implementation of curricula
at various levels within a society, the preparation of teachers, administrators and
others involved in the instructional process,
as well as the monitoring of the implementation process, the latter being in reality an
aspect of evaluation. Appendix 3 presents the
detailed analysis of components of the curriculum, made available to participants in the
project (2).

Curriculum Evaluation

"Evaluation" refers to a process involving (a) an initial

experience of "finding-out" which is (b) interpreted by means of standards, rules, or principles, in order to (c) arrive at a judgment of goodness or desirability (3). In this sense evaluation is an essential regulating mechanism in everyday life. It is a means by which individuals and groups constantly interpret their own experience for the purpose of shaping future experience.

Educational evaluation tends to be associated with change, innovation, and growth. It may focus on the needs and accomplishments of learners themselves in order to facilitate decisions that affect those learners directly. Alternatively, evaluation may assess the effectiveness or desirability of any conditions that affect learning. *Curriculum evaluation* belongs in the latter category. It is concerned with the effectiveness of all conditions, both planned and unplanned, that potentially have an influence on learning.

Much evaluation in education is informal and impressionistic, rather than systematic and objective. But whatever its nature, evaluation is so embedded in educational practice that it is unnecessary to make a case for its importance. Rather, the real concern is that evaluation be conducted in a manner that is both constructive and relevant. Evaluation must be adaptive to the values and philosophy underlying a given educational process. It must address criteria that are important to the case in question. The exploration of evaluative criteria is a way of becoming more precise about what is relevant and important in the perspective of lifelong education.

The domain of phenomena comprising curriculum as defined in this project was very broad. However, it is difficult to see how a more restricted approach could have been taken given the very inclusive nature of the lifelong education concept. The scope of activity comprising curriculum evaluation must therefore be correspondingly inclusive. Distinctions are needed which clarify both the special qualities of evaluation as well as the differences between it and other, related activities.

Scriven's (1967) distinction between *formative* and *summative* evaluation has had an important influence on the way in which those responsible for curriculum evaluation conceive of their professional roles. Formative evaluation is concerned with the improvement of an on-going educational activity. It implies direct involvement on the part of the evaluator, is very often informal, and emphasizes feedback to those who are responsible for developing and implementing the curriculum. Formative evaluation tends to focus on aspects of an educational process rather than on that process as a whole.

Summative evaluation is generally undertaken to obtain an appraisal of the overall worth of a curriculum. The recipients of summative evaluation reports are usually somewhat removed from the level of the classroom or school and are often primarily concerned with the allocation of resources rather than with the everyday process of teaching and learning. While Cronbach (1963) has been quite sceptical about the relative worth of summative evaluation in terms of its real potential for improving education, Scriven (1967) sees it standing as an equal partner with formative evaluation. Aspects of the latter relating to the teaching/learning process have been elaborated by Bloom et al. (1971). The national evaluation studies summarized in this report are all of the summative variety.

To attempt to encompass the variety of functions that make up evaluation in a single definition would be counter-productive. Rather, it seems wiser to establish critical characteristics which contrast curriculum evaluation against the broader, but partly overlapping, domain that is educational research in general. The more applicable to a given activity that each of the following characteristics may be, the more purely "evaluative" will be that activity.

Evaluation in education always entails an appraisal of the desirability of events, conditions, or states associated with learning and teaching. Evaluation is empirical in its basic approach to knowledge. It involves collecting, organizing and interpreting information about events associated with the educational process.

In order to render an appraisal of desirability, evaluation must refer to a value system that defines what is, and what is not, desirable. Values are adopted, whether consciously or unconsciously, on the bases of philosophical and ethical considerations rather than in recognition of empirical or pragmatic truths. Different societies or sub-societies may choose initially to interpret principles of lifelong education in different ways and as a result may use different criteria for appraising the desirability of whatever events are observed. As time passes, the building of a "learning society" would presumably lead to harmonization of criteria applied in different societies. In any case, the choice of evaluative criteria represents the concretization of values and should be seen as the most critical aspect of any evaluation.

Evaluation is typically a field activity in that the information it utilizes is collected mainly in situations where international learning activities occur in their natural settings. Evaluation derives generalizations from the real world of educational practice rather than from the controlled conditions of the experimental laboratory.

The practice of evaluation ordinarily does not achieve the kind of control over the conditions being studied that could be exercised, for example, by social scientists working in an experimental context. This suggests that evaluation is likely to be most useful when those who are responsible are close to the phenomena being assessed. Unanticipated consequences of real educational activities are probably the rule rather than the exception. But such consequences may not be noticed unless evaluators are in a position to notice them.

Because of the frequent lack of experimental control and the likelihood of unforeseen events and consequences, evaluative information is often more difficult to interpret than is information generated in controlled educational research. On the other hand, conclusions derived from evaluation may in many instances be more generalizable because they are derived from "real", rather than artificial, situations. Most educational ideas and innovations can work under some set of ideal conditions. Generalization in the real world requires testing in that world. This latter observation, of course, applies to summative, rather than formative, curriculum evaluation. Formative evaluation is by definition concerned with the here and now of a particular educational programme or other activity.

Evaluation is always undertaken to facilitate decision-making or policy formulation. This principle may appear to be something of a truism, but it needs to be reiterated because educational research, especially in its "pure" form, may legitimately be undertaken for the sake of contributing to knowledge and without any particular decision situations in mind. Since evaluation takes time and uses up resources, it cannot afford to engage in the collection of information for its own sake. Evaluations have to be planned and carried out with a utilitarian bias as to the nature of the information collected. At the same time, evaluations may be worse than useless when so rigidly planned and structured that unanticipated events and consequences are not detected. In this regard, Scriven (1972) has even advocated the concept of "goal-free" evaluation. He suggests that pre-stated goals and objectives often do not correspond to the actual educational activities that eventually result. Evaluators ought therefore to avoid the biases generated by knowledge of such goals and instead observe the educational activities themselves in order to deduce what is really intended and accomplished by participants in the educational process.

Next Steps

The chapter that follows describes the conclusions of the first meeting with the national teams, details the development and revision of the criteria at the national level, and presents the final list of combined criteria in illustrative form. The fifth chapter describes the procedures and illustrative results of the documentary and empirical evaluation studies of national curricula using the national criteria. Its primary emphasis is on comparing alternative methods for applying the criteria to the evaluation of national curricula in the perspective of lifelong education, rather than on making comparisons between national curricula. The sixth chapter summarizes suggestions for improving the national curricula derived from the three reports, and the last chapter summarizes the project as a whole.

NOTES

1. Taken from the summary report of the Meeting of Experts on the Content of Education in the Context of Lifelong Education. *Final Report*. Paris: UNESCO, 20-25 October, 1975. (Annex II).

2. In a personal communication based on their review of this report in draft form Professors Gestrelius and Frederiksson of the Swedish team correctly point out that the six categories of curriculum components do not necessarily make it clear that the organization of a school as, for example, a uniform comprehensive school with several choices of tracks, freedom in making such choices, and the chance to change from one track to another is also part of the curriculum. "Since the actual organization of the school can be

regarded as being important for the development of
lifelong education it is essential that this should
be clear." This point is certainly well-taken, especially since the first two criterion clusters to
be described in the next chapter deal with organizational and structural factors in schooling.
3. Much of this discussion is summarized from the afore-
mentioned work by Skager (1977).

REFERENCES

Bloom, B.; Hastings, J.I. and Madaus, G.I. *Handbook on
Formative and Summative Evaluation of Student Learning*. New York: McGraw Hill, 1971.

Cronbach, L.J. "Course Improvement through Evaluation".
Teachers College Record, 64, 1963, pp.672-683.

Dave, R.H. *Reflections on Lifelong Education and the
School*. UIE Monograph 3. Hamburg: Unesco Institute
for Education, 1975.

Payne, D.A. *Curriculum Evaluation*. Lexington, Massa-
chusetts: D.C. Heath, 1974.

Popham, W.J. (ed.). *Evaluation in Education*. Berkeley,
California: McCutchan, 1974.

Scriven, M. "The Methodology of Evaluation". In Tyler,
R.; Gagné, R. and Scriven, M. *Perspectives of Curriculum Evaluation*. Chicago: Rand McNally, 1967,
pp.39-83.

Scriven, M. "Pros and Cons about Goal-Free Evaluation".
Evaluation Comment. Center for the Study of Evalua-
tion. Los Angeles: University of California, 3,
No. 4, 1972, pp.1-4.

Skager, R.W. *Evaluation and Lifelong Learning*. Hamburg:
Unesco Institute for Education, 1977.

Worthen, B.R. and Sanders, J.R. *Educational Evaluation:
Theory and Practice*. Belmont, California: C.A. Jones,
1973.

CHAPTER 4

DEVELOPMENT OF THE EVALUATIVE CRITERIA

Criteria may be defined as standards against which phenomena are judged or appraised. They are derived from value based
conceptualizations which are normative in the sense of specifying a desired state of affairs. Criteria also reflect whatever
a given conceptualization or theory holds to be important. They
are selective in the sense of calling attention to the special
significance of a subset of phenomena that make up a larger,
more complex entity. It is even conceivable that sets of criteria derived from different conceptualizations of what is desirable educationally might refer to entirely different aspects
of whatever is being evaluated.

New conceptualizations of education stimulate the reformu-
lation of evaluative criteria. This process often involves the
interpretation of principles stated at a somewhat abstract
level. When the conceptualization is very inclusive and stated
at a high level of abstraction it is likely that somewhat different interpretations may be made by different individuals,
especially if those individuals come from different intellectual and cultural traditions.

Lifelong education was described earlier as a "master
concept" incorporating a set of highly inclusive principles,
formulated so as to encompass the totality of educational en-
deavour. As a framework (that is receiving a great deal of attention internationally), it is open to variation in interpretation by individuals with different perceptions of the meaning
of the principles and manner of their application. This is especially true when attempts are made to state specific evaluative criteria. We are of course interested in the differences
that emerge from particular national perspectives as to how
evaluative criteria are to be stated. But we are also interested in communalities that may emerge, as well as in the level of
specification at which general agreement on criteria is possible.

This chapter describes the process by which the three national teams working in cooperation with the staff of an international institute went about the development and refinement of
criteria to be used for judging the strengths and limitations
of school curricula from the perspective of lifelong education.
It provides examples of particular criteria stressed by individual national teams as well as a list of combined criteria at
various levels of specificity.

Sources

The twenty concept characteristics listed in Appendix 2
were described as a starting point for the development of the
evaluative criteria of this report. Their influence will be especially apparent in the basic categories under which the criteria have been grouped. However, the concept clusters are not
the only written source from which criteria were derived. For
example, a position paper prepared by the Co-Director of the
Japanese team had considerable influence on the Japanese study.
Professor Masui's proposal is summarized in the Japanese national report. It emphasized "growth and "time" as two principles underlying lifelong education. The growth principle was
characterized as the most fundamental of the two, referring to
(a) continuous development in the individual of a "progressive"
value system and (b) development in the individual of an attitude of responsibility for his own learning. The time principle,
derived from the first, eschews the image of education as "preparation" and defines the essential purpose of lifelong education as one of developing

"... a person who endeavours to achieve *self-
growth* or *self-formation* throughout his life".

The emphasis on *growth* criteria was readily apparent in the
list of criteria developed by the Japanese national team.

The Romanian national report surveyed the foundations of
lifelong education in terms of several trends:

a) *psychological*, especially the need for continuing intellectual development;

b) *socio-practical*, or the integration of work
and learning activities;

c) *culturological*, or the use of the increasing
spare-time available to individuals in de-

veloped societies, and

d) *futurological*, or utilizing the capacity of the scientific and technological revolution in the transformation of society.

The Swedish report turned to psychological learning theory, citing the literature pertaining to motivational factors in learning, especially the role of curiosity, imitation and play in the enhancement of satisfaction on the part of learners. The Swedish criteria, as will be seen, were derived so as to reflect as closely as possible Dave's (1973) concept characteristics (Appendix 2).

Each of the national teams assessed the needs to be fulfilled under lifelong education in a manner that was at least in part unique. All started from the same point, but rather clearly expressed their own perspectives in the national reports. These perspectives were extended into the actual process of deriving and refining the criteria at the national level.

Processes for Deriving Initial Multinational Criteria

Development of specific evaluative criteria for this research began with parallel analyses into

a) the implications of the concept characteristics of lifelong education and

b) the basic operational components of any curriculum, the latter described in the previous chapter.

These two analyses ultimately led to a kind of conceptual grid (Appendix 5) which facilitated the development of evaluative criteria.

A list of seven implications of the concept characteristics of lifelong education served as a starting point:

1) School curricula should regard learning processes as continuous, occurring from early childhood to late adulthood. Vertical articulation between different stages of learning, aspects of human development and changing roles at different stages of life should be established.

2) School curricula should be viewed in the context of concurrent learning processes going
   on in the home, community, place of work, etc.

3) The importance of essential unity of knowledge
   and interrelationship between different subjects of study must be kept in view while re-
   forming school curricula.

4) The school is one of the chief agencies for
   providing basic education within the framework of lifelong education. School curricula
   reflect this specific function of the school.

5) School education controls to a large extent
   the education that occurs during later life.
   Therefore, school curricula should emphasize
   auto-didactics including self-learning and
   inter-learning, development of educability
   and readiness for further learning, and cultivation of learning attitudes appropriate to
   the needs of a changing society.

6) School curricula should take into account the
   need for establishing and renewing a progressive value system by individuals so that they
   can take their own responsibilities for continuous growth throughout life.

7) School curricula should provide historical as
   well as contemporary perspectives of life and
   help understand divergent value systems.

The above implications were a first step in the deriva-
tion of more specific criteria. As just indicated, the process
of deriving criteria also took into account the specific components of the curriculum described in the previous chapter. Appendix 3 reproduces the original list of components and sub-
components used in the first workshop. It will be recalled
that the six components were labelled:

1) Objectives

2) Curriculum Plan

3) Teaching Methods and Learning Activities

4) Learning Materials

5) Evaluation Procedures

6) Curriculum Implementation.

During the first international workshop the development
of the initial list of evaluative criteria proceeded in two
stages. In the first stage the implications listed above were
used to generate sets of goals for each of the six curriculum
components. For example, the curriculum component *Objectives*
was elaborated into some fifteen goal areas such as "Co-ordination with the home", "Co-ordination with the local community",
"Articulation with the pre-school experience", etc. The complete set of goals for the objectives component is provided in
Appendix 4. Each of the fifteen goals was further elaborated by
several explanatory statements. Thus, for "Co-ordination with
the home", the following statements were listed:

1) Complementary roles of the home and the school.

2) Unique role and responsibility of the school
   in the context of the home.

3) Preparation for future parental role.

4) Parental involvement in daily programme of
   the school.

5) Parental involvement in the development of the
   school programme.

6) Recognition of the need to provide mechanisms
   to co-ordinate home with school.

The above explanatory statements, like the many others
that were developed at this stage of the research do not com-
prise "criteria" as the term was defined earlier. That is, the
statements were not cast in a form that incorporates actual
standards of judgment. But they are perhaps not far removed
from the stage of specification of standards and certainly
would facilitate the development of the latter.

It is encouraging that statements like the above were mutually acceptable to participants representing different cultures and social systems. Of course sectional differences would
undoubtedly emerge if, for example, the *exact nature* of parental participation and involvement in the school were spelled
out in the form of standards for evaluative judgment. This in
no way detracts from the fact that the lifelong education framework did provide grounds on which educators from different societies could achieve consensus.

The second stage of elaboration involved the development
of overall categories or clusters of evaluative criteria general

enough to be applicable to all curriculum components. Each combination of criterion category and curriculum component defined
a cluster of more specific criteria. The resulting matrix reproduced in Appendix 5 influenced the later national reports,
especially that produced by the Romanian team. It should be
noted that in Appendix 5 the curriculum component *Learning Materials* does not appear as it was combined for this particular
table with the category of *Teaching Methods and Learning Activities*. The clusters of evaluative criteria can be defined as
follows:

Horizontal Integration

Criteria subsumed under this cluster stress the building
of relationships between schools and all other social institutions and structures having a potential educational function.
This implies recognition that what is learned in schools com-
prises only a part of the total learning of individuals in any
society and calls for a systematization and coordination of the
school curriculum with non-school educational opportunities. In
a parallel fashion it also calls for integration of the subject
matter at any given level.

Vertical Articulation

This second cluster is a logical counterpart of the first
in emphasizing a second type of linkage, one which connects educational delivery systems oriented to differing age levels in
the population, especially the pre-school, school and post-
school learning phases. It places a correlated emphasis on linkages within subjects or other curriculum domains that cut across
institutional levels such as grades or levels of schooling.

Individual and Collective Growth

This category subsumes criteria relating to personal and
collective growth, especially in the area of the development of
values and social, emotional, intellectual, and physical aspects
of the individual. It is not tied closely to subject matter or
curriculum in the traditional sense, but rather reflects concern with broader, maturational aspects of personal development.

Auto-Didactic (Self-Directed Learning)

The fourth category of criteria is logically related to
the one that precedes it. It focusses on the development of characteristics or processes in learners that contribute to personal growth. Here the emphasis is on "learning to learn", either

as an individual or as a member of a cooperative social entity. There is a clear implication that individuals exemplifying patterns of lifelong learning would manifest a high degree of autonomy and independence in their role as learners, and the ability to utilize any and all learning modes, including guidance by others, is seen as highly desirable.

Other Aspects

A number of potentially important criteria were grouped in what at first appeared to be a miscellaneous cluster. These included flexibility and adaptability in the curriculum, the encouragement of innovativeness or creativity, and the provision for a diversity of approach to fit the diversity that typically exists among learners. Further development of this last set of criteria at the national and the final multinational phases later revealed an underlying unity. This unity turned out to be expressed most fully under the label "democratization".

The above summarizes results of the deliberations of the participants during the first multinational stage of the research. For each curriculum component an extensive and differentiated list of goals and explanatory statements has been developed from implications deducted from the concept characteristics of lifelong education. In addition, a clustering of potential evaluative criteria across the various curriculum components had been achieved. These were the raw materials with which the national teams began their work.

Processes for Deriving National Evaluative Criteria

Each of the national teams engaged in an extensive process of reviewing and refining the criteria developed during the planning phase. This process involved both empirical and logical analyses. While all of the possible methods for developing criteria for evaluating national curricula could not be exhausted in a three nation study, the approaches summarized here have both differences and communalities that serve to illustrate the variety of alternative approaches that are available.

Pilot Content Analysis

The Swedish and Romanian teams began the development of national criterion lists by conducting a pilot content analysis of parts of the written curriculum. In this exercise misclassifications of particular criteria from the initial list, overlap between different criterion categories, lack of clarity in the meaning of particular statements, and the like, were identified and corrected.

The Swedish team used the following procedure. The slightly modified initial criterion list was divided into the five major clusters described above, with the fifth or general cluster reformulated somewhat to reflect an emphasis on "equality and critical thinking". Each cluster was further subdivided into sub-clusters containing a number of explanatory statements which suggested evaluative criteria. For example, the first cluster *Horizontal Integration* was divided into seven sub-clusters, the first of which was "Integration School-Home". Explanatory statements under this sub-cluster included

"Giving the parents information and the opportunity of stating their views on the implementation of a new curriculum";

"active cooperation of the parents in planning the daily programme of their children", etc.

These and other statements defined the meaning of each sub-cluster for use in the pilot curriculum analysis.

The two numbers of the Swedish team then independently read through the basic school curriculum plan once for one sub-cluster. For example, the entire curriculum was read for evidence of "Horizontal Integration, School-Home" (the example just given). The judges then moved to "School-Society", the next sub-cluster of *Horizontal Integration*, and so on. Each section of the curriculum text judged to pertain to the criterion sub-category was so marked. This was done in a highly analytical fashion, sentence by sentence, and at times even in sentences fragment by fragment, where more than one criterion applied to a given sentence. For the first three criterion clusters all of the initial sub-categories were used. Some combinations were made among sub-categories for the last two categories.

The above process with the basic school curriculum was repeated with upper secondary materials. By this time the two judges were so familiar with the categories that each text needed to be read only five times, or once for each of the major criterion clusters rather than once for each of the sub-clusters.

At this point the question of *inter-judge agreement* naturally arose. That is, if the explanatory statements were useful as criteria applicable to a written curriculum, then judges working independently ought to achieve the same or very similar classifications of the curriculum *vis à vis* the five major criterion clusters. If this was not the case then modifications in the criteria and/or changes of the judgmental procedures would have to be made in order to achievè an appropriate level of reliability.

Studies of inter-judge agreement were made both at the beginning of the judgments and again after all judgments were completed. The procedure used does not demand technical competency in complex statistical procedures, yet it provided useful information. Because the matter of interjudge agreement is very important in any attempt at the content analysis, an example will be taken from the Swedish report.

In this particular analysis a section of the basic school curriculum was selected in order to compare the way in which the two judges applied the "Integration School-Society" sub-category of the *Horizontal Integration* cluster. It turned out that the judges working independently had classified 74 and 70 sentences or sentence fragments, respectively, as referring to integration of school and society. A precise description of the manner in which the implications of the comparison were explored is contained in the Swedish report. (In the exerpt quoted below the term "unit" refers to a sentence or sentence fragment and "A" and "B" to the first and second judge.)

> "A lacked 9 of the units extracted by B, while B
> lacked 11 of A's. A total of 83 units had been
> extracted of which 63 (76%) agreed. When the
> units extracted by A and B were compared, it
> was found that on a few occasions one evaluator
> had a single unit that corresponded to two (and
> in one case even three) units of the other ...
> After discussions between the evaluators while
> the work was underway, it was decided to make
> the units large enough to prevent any misunder-
> standing about the content of the unit arising
> in the second check ..." (p.25).

The results of this pilot work showed that criteria belonging to the clusters of *Horizontal Integration* and *Vertical Articulation* could be applied with a high level of agreement

among judges. There was a less satisfactory pattern of agreement for the other three clusters. The judges reported that
here an uncomfortable degree of subjectivity entered into the
interpretation of possibly pertinent statements in the curriculum and advised more caution in interpreting the findings for
these clusters.

The Swedish team then developed a final list of criteria
based on their experience in the pilot content analysis. The
five main clusters were retained, but some of the subdivisions
were moved to different clusters. Many overlapping criterion
statements were combined to drastically reduce the number of
statements. In the end the criterion list contained 26 "sub-
criteria" for the five clusters, with these sub-criteria elaborated by a total of 81 "definitions". (The sub-criteria rather
than the definitions constituted the units of analysis in the
content analyses reported in the next chapter.)

The Romanian team did not conduct a formal content analysis, although portions of the curriculum were broken down into
units as a starting point in developing the criteria. A set of
"analytical cards" was constructed, each listing a statement
taken from governmental educational regulations and related
specialized educational literature. The six curriculum components of Chapter 3 were reduced to four: Objectives, Programmes,
Methods, and Systems of Evaluation. Statements from the above
documents reflecting one of the four components were then entered onto the cards. Interviews in schools were also conducted
to obtain statements describing the curriculum.

The preliminary table of criteria was organized into five
main content categories corresponding fairly closely to the
original clustered characteristics of lifelong education:

1) School-Society Relations

2) Preparation and Achievement of Lifelong Education along the School Levels

3) Development of Personality

4) Learning and Self-Learning

5) Creativity.

Each of these categories was further broken down into sub-
categories, again with some modification of the original planning session list. Finally, criterion statements corresponding

to each of the four curriculum components were selected or developed within each sub-cluster. The preliminary set of Romanian criteria thus reflected reasonably closely the categories of the planning session (see Appendix 5), but drew heavily from local sources for more specific criterion statements. Use by the Romanians of the double classification system of (a) components of the curriculum and (b) clustered characteristics of lifelong education resulted in the most lengthy and detailed list of evaluative criteria of the three national studies.

Judgments of Teachers, Students and Parents

The preliminary list of Romanian criteria was made available to a large number of research workers, teachers and administrators. Their more or less informal comments were used to revise the list. During this process the number of criteria was reduced from 185 to 140 statements. An effort was also made by members of the team to judge the measurability of the criteria, although lack of measurability did not constitute sole grounds for removing a criterion from the list.

The final input to the revision of the criteria came from formal evaluations by teachers in the four schools included in the research sample (described in the next chapter). While the number of schools was not large, they were varied in location and level. For this purpose "Scales of Evaluation" were developed for obtaining ratings of selected criterion statements on each of four dimensions:

1) *Applicability*, or the possibility of applying the criterion statement taking into account the nature of the school and level and type of training of the teaching staff.

2) *Relevancy*, or importance assigned to the particular criterion.

3) *Efficiency*, or "productivity" of the criterion if applied in the sense of economic and functional impact.

4) *Clearness*, or, in the text of the Romanian report, "... whether the respective criteria are expressed in proper terms, whether they are accessible and transmissible to other members of the didactic staff without additional explanation" (p.39).

The ratings themselves were on a three point scale. The subset of criterion statements selected for this process numbered 37 and was representative of most of the categories of the total list of criteria.

Generally speaking, the results of this particular study revealed that the teaching staff sampled was especially concerned about the dimensions of efficiency and applicability. In a number of instances the clarity of particular statements was also questioned. These results were used in a final stage of revision of the table of criteria.

Analytical Empirical Procedures

The Japanese team in a number of respects took a different approach to the development of evaluative criteria. For one thing, the Japanese conducted the most extensive restructuring in the material developed at the initial meeting of participants. The number of criteria was drastically reduced by writing the statements at more general level. Likewise, the clustering of criteria was significantly reorganized.

This restructuring had its origin in two factors. First, as already noted, the philosophical orientation under which the team worked stressed the concept of personal growth as central to the framework of lifelong education.

"We think that the most important thing is that aspect of the personality system indicated by the concept (of) 'personal growth'. Consequently, we feel that formal education should be evaluated in terms of criteria that are directly related to individual personal growth in the above sense " (p.84).

This emphasis on individual growth is reflected in the first two of the five clusters of Japanese criteria:

1) Development of a Sound Attitude toward Self-Learning

2) Development of Learning Skills

3) Encouragement of Flexible Teaching

4) Horizontal Integration in Teaching

5) Vertical Articulation in Teaching

Each of the clusters was elaborated with from three to seven statements. For example, under the first or "Self-Learning" cluster there were four statements, the first being,

"Cultivation of intrinsic interest in learning".

In all, there were 25 criterion statements under the five main headings. A sixth or miscellaneous category was also utilized although its content was only illustrated in the English language report.

The second basis for the restructuring of the criterion list had to do with the way in which the Japanese planned to utilize it in the study. The general statements listed above were not really intended as criteria, but rather as guidelines for the development of *criterion instruments* such as questionnaires, interview schedules, and the like. While the Romanian team also used their criterion list to developing measuring instruments, the Japanese placed by far the greatest emphasis on the development of measurement procedures and the analysis of empirical data derived through the use of those procedures.

The Japanese also viewed the development of criteria as at least in part an empirical process. The construction of criterion measures ordinarily involves collecting and analyzing empirical data. Information derived from criterion instruments themselves or from other sources of data can be used in modifying or elaborating the criteria those instruments were designed to measure. For this reason the criterion list just discussed was treated in the Japanese report as a highly tentative initial step subject to revision on the basis of empirical findings.

Although the chapter which follows will outline the major empirical studies of the three national reports, at least one of those studies is also relevant here. It was conducted by the Japanese partly with the object of providing information that might be used in later revisions of the criterion list. The study was designed to explore what was termed the "structure" of the personal growth variables. In other words, its object was to determine empirically the major dimensions by which personal growth can be defined and measured.

Using the first two criterion clusters as guidelines, two student questionnaires were developed. The first was structured around attitudes relating to personal growth. It consisted of 48 questions to be answered by the respondent in terms of applicability to the self. A three-choice response format was used

("Yes, No, I don't know"). Sample questions will be given below in relationship to the actual findings. The second questionnaire described 11 different types of self-educative activity that might be engaged in by learners. We are interested only in the first questionnaire at this point.

The questionnaire on personal growth was given to a group of 540 pupils made up of 45 boys and 45 girls from one elementary, lower secondary, and upper secondary school in an urban and in a rural setting (total of 6 schools). Responses to the items were intercorrelated and factor analyzed for

a) the total sample,
b) boys only, and
c) girls only.

As with any other factor analysis, the purpose here was one of simplification and organization (1). The object was to identify clusters of items that individual respondents tended to answer in the same way and that could as a result be taken as defining general dimensions used by learners in describing their own growth characteristics. These dimensions in turn suggest empirically based growth criteria.

The analysis of the total sample yielded four factors listed below under the labels provided in the Japanese report. One representative questionnaire item will be provided for each factor:

Factor 1: *Confidence/Self-Acceptance*
"unsure of myself" (negative factor leading)

Factor 2: *Achievement Motivation*
"want to succeed in what others can't do"

Factor 3: *Dependence on External Judgment*
"concerned about what other people say about me"

Factor 4: *Desire and Efforts for Improvement*
"always finish what I have decided to do".

The Japanese report went on to use results of the factor analyses in arriving at some tentative conclusions about the impact of the school curricula, and these will be discussed in the next chapter. For the present, the structure identified suggests that the students were able to describe their own personal growth status in terms of four differentiated aspects of the self. These findings suggest possible revisions or further specifications of the initial list of growth criteria.

Summary

The three national teams, while starting from the same point, each used different approaches to the development of national lists of criteria for evaluating school curricula. The Swedes elaborated on the original criteria, producing a long initial list which was in turn revised and shortened on the basis of experience during the pilot content analysis of statements abstracted from the written curriculum. The Romanians did something similar, though in a less quantitative fashion, but placed more stress on obtaining ratings from teachers on various aspects of the criteria. The Japanese to some extent reconceptualized lifelong education (growth and time dimensions) and produced an initial list of criteria in part reflecting their own emphasis. The Japanese especially regarded their list as only a first step subject to revision on the basis of research findings and further conceptual work.

The Romanian criterion list contained the greatest number of statements, probably because it retained the original dual differentiation provided by clustered concept characteristics of lifelong education and components of the curriculum (Appendix 5). The other two teams constructed their criterion lists to reflect characteristics of lifelong education which were pertinent to all components of the curriculum. Of these the Swedish list was the longer and more specific. The Japanese was by far the shortest and more general of the three lists, although its real specification was in the criterion instruments developed for the empirical studies conducted by this national team. In spite of modifications in emphasis and specificity at the national level similarities in the criterion lists were readily apparent. These served as the basis for the development of a combined list in the second and final multinational meeting.

Developing the Combined List of Criteria

A good deal of the discussion in the second meeting of the participants in the study was devoted to the development of a combined list of criteria. This process involved five stages of work.

    1) A sample table was constructed for comparison
       purpose which listed at the left hand margin
       the original 15 categories of criteria devel-

oped at the first joint meeting for the objectives curriculum component. These are reproduced in Appendix 4. In three columns to the
right of this list corresponding criteria from
the national reports were entered whenever applicable. Thus, for the first criterion category of the initial session, "Co-ordination
with the Home", the Japanese equivalent was
"Involvement of the Parents in Teaching Activities", the Romanian "School-Family Relationships", and the Swedish "Integration of
School and Home". While some of the category
labels did not correspond so closely across
the initial and three national lists, it was
clear to the participants that sufficient com-
munality still existed to provide the basis
for developing a combined list based on the
three national studies.

2) Next, the four major clusters of criteria were
in part redefined on the basis of the national
work and listed as *Horizontal Integration, Vertical Articulation, Orientations to Self-Growth*
(from the earlier cluster, "Individual and Collective Growth"), and *Self-Directed Learning*
(from the earlier, "Auto-Didactic"). At this
point the fifth category still remained unde-
fined in any overall sense. Each criterion
cluster was dealt with separately. In joint
session, the participants discussed and agreed
upon a mutually acceptable list of first level
"elaborations" (in a later stage referred to
as "criteria") on each cluster. Thus, for
Self-Directed Learning five elaborations were
finally agreed upon:
  - Participation in the planning, execution
    and evaluation of learning
  - Individualization of learning
  - Development of skills of self-learning
  - Development of skills of inter-learning
  - Development of skills of self-evaluation
    and co-operative evaluation.

3) Two-column work sheets listing the initial elaborations for each criterion cluster on the
left were made up and distributed to each national team. Their task, working separately,

was to provide a list of "specifications" for
each elaboration. For example, one of the elaborations for the *Vertical Articulation* cluster was, "Integration between different grades/
levels". For this particular statement the
Swedish team developed three specifications:

a) Organization of the school as a united,
   basic school instead of as a parallel
   school system.

b) Measures for aiding the continuity of
   the students' studies and promoting
   a smooth transference between the
   levels.

c) Linkage between organization and study
   content of different school levels.

This process, then, ended with three national lists of specifications for each elaborative
statement of the four criterion clusters. This
material provided the basis for the final collective effort at generating a single set of
criteria.

4) When the national teams had completed their
   list of specifications for each of the four
   defined clusters the participants met again
   in joint session to combine them into a single
   set. It proved to be relatively easy to do
   this as far as the content of the specifications was concerned. Most of the discussion
   centered on the meaning of terms and on the
   formulation of common wording for similar specifications produced by different teams. In
   spite of the fact that national perspectives
   had demonstrably entered into the form and
   content of the criterion lists for each country, it was still possible to move back to a
   multinational list. While the relative emphasis of the different teams may not have been
   the same, there were virtually no instances
   in which the criterion specifications from
   one country were not acceptable in principle
   to participants from other countries.

5) The final step in the refinement of the lifelong education criteria occurred after the
   second joint session and in part involved

editing and writing by UIE staff members who
had participated in the study. One major addition was made at this stage. Re-examination
of the fifth or miscellaneous criterion cluster, which had not really been attended to
systematically during the second joint session,
appeared to reveal an underlying unity reflecting in various ways the idea of "democratization", a concept commonly referred to
in the literature on lifelong education. The
cluster was renamed and expanded under the
general heading of *Democratization.* As will be
seen in the criteria themselves, this broad
concept reflects themes relating to equality
of opportunity, participation by learners in
decision-making, humanization of inter-person-
al relationships, especially relations between
persons of different status, and, in the learning process itself, encouragement of indivi-
duality, divergent thinking, curiosity, and
creativity. Finally, this cluster of criteria
also incorporates themes commonly expressed in
lifelong education relating to the principle
of equality, especially in the sense of extending equal opportunity to all. All of these
themes can be summarized under the *Democrati-*
zation cluster incorporating many of the central concerns of many writers on lifelong education.

Combined Evaluative Criteria

The combined criterion list is only a first step in the
development of criteria for evaluating curricula within the
perspective of lifelong education. All of those who participated in its preparation recognized the need for further elaboration and development. The list is meant to stimulate further
work.

The combined criterion list is ordered into three levels
of specificity. At the most general level we have the five
clusters or categories: *Horizontal Integration, Vertical Artic-*
ulation, Orientation to Self-Growth, Self-Directed Learning,
and *Democratization.* These clusters represent a very high level
of abstraction and appear to be adequately inclusive of the

principles of lifelong education as they relate to curriculum. The clusters as principles thus would appear to be unlikely to undergo radical modification.

At the second level are lists of *criteria* referring to desirable states or conditions implied by the definition of each cluster. Our experience suggests that these statements will be widely acceptable as accurate reflections of the basic principles of lifelong education. Without doubt additional statements at this level will be proposed and incorporated, and in this sense the criteria are more susceptible to modification and extension than are the clusters under which they are classified.

At the third level two or more *specifications* were developed for each criterion statement. Many of these statements are sufficiently specific to have the potential for stimulating debate about appropriateness and desirability. It is likely that their application in any national context would result in at least some significant changes in wording as well as omissions and additions. The specifications elaborating the criteria sometimes reflect the particular concerns of a single national team. This is as it should be. The lists of specifications are offered as open categories. New statements can be added. Existing statements should be used where they apply and ignored where they are inappropriate or cannot be applied.

It will be clear from the criteria listed below that further levels of specification would have to be undertaken in order to arrive at descriptions of actual curriculum components and evaluation instruments. While this could not be done at the multinational level, illustrations of how to conduct this process will be given after presentation of the criteria and illustrative specifications. A full list of combined criteria and the specifications appears in Appendix 6.

Combined List of Criteria and Illustrative Specifications

I. *Horizontal Integration*

Functional integration of all social agencies fulfilling educational functions, as well as among elements of the curriculum at any given level and among learners with different personal characteristics.

Criteria and Illustrative Specifications:

1) Integration between school and home

> School and home maintain complementary roles in education of the child.

2) Integration between school and community (local, national, international)

> Community facilities, resources and experience are used for school activities.

3) Integration between school and world of work

> School activities are related to actual production through study visits and trained periods at different places of work.

4) Integration between school and cultural institutions, organizations and activities

> Films, theatre, music, museums, libraries and sport are incorporated in the school curriculum.

5) Integration between school and mass media

> Ability is developed in learners to evaluate critically information presented via mass media.

6) Integration of subjects of study

> Different school subjects are integrated into wider fields of study.

7) Integration between curricula subjects and extra-curricular activities

> Learners acquire skills for use in leisure.

8) Integration of learners having different characteristics

> Learners of different ethnic, physical, intellectual, religious, and social characteristics jointly participate in the learning process.

II. *Vertical Articulation*

Articulation among curriculum components at different levels of schooling and between school curricula and pre- and post-school education.

Criteria and Illustrative Specifications:

1) Integration between pre-school experiences and the school

   Interest in future school learning is awakened with visits to school and other extra curricular incentives.

2) Integration between different grades or other levels within the school

   Organization and study content at different school levels are linked systematically.

3) Integration between school and post-school activities

   Learners are informed about organization, operation and entrance requirements of different forms of post-school education.

III. *Orientation to Self-Growth*

Development in learners of personal characteristics that contribute to a long-term process of growth and development including realistic self-awareness, interest in the world and in other people, the desire to achieve, internalized criteria for making evaluations and judgments, and overall integration of the personality.

Criteria and Illustrative Specifications:

1) Self-understanding

   Learners are aware of responsibility for own growth.

2) Interest in human beings and in environmental world

   Learners are interested in physical and biological environment.

3) Achievement motivation

   Learners are motivated to improve their own abilities (cognitive, affective and psychomotor).

4) Establishment of internal judgment criteria

Learners are able to formulate opinions independently.

5) Establishment of progressive values and attitudes

Learners develop flexible thinking and tolerance.

6) Integration of personality

Learners explore and assimilate an ideal model for personal development.

IV. *Self-Directed Learning*

Individualization of the learning experience toward the goal of developing the learner's own skills and competencies in the planning, execution and evaluation of learning activities both as an individual and as a member of a cooperative learning group.

Criteria and Illustrative Specifications:

1) Participation in the planning, execution, and evaluation of learning

Learners are involved in planning both school and out-of-school activities.

2) Individualization of learning

Organizational facilities are provided for making individualized teaching and learning practicable

3) Development of self-learning skills

Opportunity is provided for use of a variety of learning sources, media and materials.

4) Development of inter-learning skills

Learners share responsibility in the teaching/learning process.

5) Development of self-evaluation and cooperative evaluation skills

Group or individual work is evaluated cooperatively.

V. *Democratization*

Equality of educational opportunity, opportunity to participate in decision-making and in the teaching/learning process
despite differences in status, the constructive exercise of
authority, and the encouragement of creativity, divergent thinking, flexibility and curiosity on the part of the learners.

Criteria and Illustrative Specifications:

1) Equality of educational opportunity for all
   regardless of personal differences

   > Opportunity is available equally regard-
   > less of sex, race, religion, social back-
   > ground and other personal characteristics.

2) Sharing of decision-making and other types of
   involvement in the teaching/learning process
   among participants with different status and
   roles *vis à vis* the school

   > Parents, community, teachers and learners
   > participate in school organization and
   > administration.

3) Constructive exercise of authority

   > Non-punitive evaluation functions and
   > methods are stressed.

4) Encouragement of creativity and flexibility

   > Free creative activity, self-expression,
   > spontaneity and originality are encouraged.

It should be pointed out that the combined list of criteria, like the national lists which preceeded it, contains two
types of statements. That is, some statements define what are
usually thought of as educational "means", while other statements refer to educational goals or "ends". Organizational and
process variables listed in the *Horizontal Integration* and
Vertical Articulation clusters are in the former category. So
too, it will be seen, are a number of the statements in the
Democratization cluster. On the other hand, the two clusters
incorporating statements defining aspects of *Self-Growth* and
Self-Directed Learning refer to educational outcomes at the
level of the learner. So do some of the statements in the *Democratization* cluster. One could thus view the criteria as combining the two dimensions of means and ends, with the former
referring to organizational and process variables that need to

be implemented in order to achieve desired types of personal development in learners. Advantages and disadvantages of this type of distinction between means and ends are discussed in Skager's (1977) monograph on evaluation for lifelong education.

Steps Toward Developing and Evaluating the Curriculum

None of the above specifications of criteria actually defines a curriculum element or indicates the nature of associated evaluation instruments or procedures. The criteria and specifications are suggestive, however, of starting points and areas of emphasis. *Democratization* criteria, especially, invite further conceptual unification. All criteria require specification and interpretation at the level of programme development. As suggested earlier, activity at this level would undoubtedly be strongly influenced by the national or regional context in which this process occurred. Thus, it may be widely agreed under V. 2) above that community, teachers, parents and learners should participate in the governance of the school. The manner in which such participation is carried out would undoubtedly show wide differences in conception and custom depending on where it occurs. It seems appropriate to comment at least briefly on how the process of further elaboration might be undertaken.

Specification by Curriculum Components

A useful approach to transforming the specifications into operational curriculum elements involves

    a) deciding which criteria can be applied to each of the curriculum components described in Chapter 3 and listed in Appendix 3, and then

    b) elaborating specifications in terms of the particular component in question.

The working document developed for the initial multinational meeting at the beginning of the project illustrated this process for each of six curriculum components, as indicated earlier in this chapter. For example, under the component *Objectives* the concept characteristic "flexibility" was elaborated in the initial working document by means of four specifications, one of which read, "Provision for local adaptation of objectives". This same concept characteristic was elaborated in different ways for the component *Curriculum Plan*. Thus, one statement under flexibility read, "Possibility of developing and following alternative curriculum plans".

The Romanian team, which produced the most detailed list of criteria at the national level, followed a very similar procedure. For each criterion cluster the various criteria were elaborated in terms of the four curriculum components *Objectives, Programmes, Methods,* and *Evaluation.* For example, the criterion cluster equivalent to *Horizontal Integration* (labelled "School-Society Relationships" on the Romanian criterion list) began with relations between school and community. This category was elaborated in four separate sections corresponding to the four curriculum components just listed. Thus, one specification of the *Programmes* component on the Romanian criteria list included the specifications, "Knowledge by Pupils of Local Realities; Integration into Local Life; Creative and Productive Participation of the Pupils in Transforming Local Life" (Romanian report, Appendix 3, p.1). The two tactics of

a) assigning criteria to components and then developing specifications appropriate to the component in question versus

b) taking one criterion statement at a time and developing specifications for each component

differ mainly in the order in which things are done. However, it is possible that some criteria apply more readily to some components of the curricula than to others. The first procedure in contrast does not assume that each and every criterion statement need be elaborated in terms of each curriculum component.

The procedures just illustrated yield specifications that are usually somewhat more concrete than those on the multinational list because they take into account particular components of the curriculum. They represent one approach to the increasingly detailed specification of evaluative criteria. However, it will be recalled that the Japanese team adopted a very different procedure in that criteria were stated at a relatively abstract level. The activity analogous to specification in the case of the Japanese study took the form of developing actual evaluation instruments from the general criteria.

Relating Criteria to Operational Practice

A different strategy for moving from the general to the specific is described in greater detail in Skager's (1977) analysis of evaluation in lifelong education. It was initially proposed during the discussion of the Japanese criteria at the final workshop, but could be readily applied to criteria from the other lists, especially those which refer to the development of various characteristics in learners that have been subsumed under the clusters of *Self-Growth* and *Self-Directed Learning*. Of the five criterion clusters, these deal mainly with desired types of outcomes in learners, while the other three incorporate mainly criteria referring to operational and organizational practices. An important function of the approach to be described is one of putting these two types of criteria together in ways that contribute to the design of curricula and to the development of relevant evaluation instruments. That is, the idea is to build plausible links between criteria referring to operational practice and criteria defining desired learner characteristics.

By way of illustration, one criterion on the Japanese list under the cluster of "Self-Learning" (corresponding in general to *Self-Directed Learning* on the multinational list) referred to the importance of establishing a sound self-concept in the learner. During the final workshop meeting the meaning of the term "self-concept" was discussed. Several elaborations were suggested, including "self-awareness", "self-confidence", and "self-acceptance". These terms of course suggest what are often referred to as "psychological constructs". That is, they are conceptual or theoretical abstractions - generalizations made in order to explain consistencies in the behaviour of individual persons or groups. Thus, people described as "self-confident" tend to display their self-confidence in a variety of situations and a variety of ways. Their behaviour and personal style is thus to some degree consistent and predictable on the basis of their standing on the construct. But the constructs cited above are still very abstract. The real need is to develop strategies for building and evaluating curricula that help develop, for example, self-confidence in learners. In other words, how do we move from criteria referring to abstract theoretical constructs down to the concrete specification of desirable curriculum components and relevant evaluative instruments?

One approach is illustrated in Figure 4.1. The three constructs referred to above are listed hierarchically as the first column. In a complete treatment each construct label would be elaborated by a detailed definition statement differentiating between behavioural manifestations of the construct and manifestations of other, related constructs. This definition would specify the kinds of behaviour that are indicative of each construct and also specify and exclude other classes

FIGURE 4.1

LINKING CRITERIA TO OPERATIONAL PRACTICES THROUGH THEORY

THEORY	DEDUCTIONS
Constructs and Related Educational Principles	Instructional Guidelines

Learners develop *Self-Aware-ness* about their own interests and capacities through experience in concrete situations. →

Learners should always receive accurate feedback as to the quality of their performance in any learning situation.

Learners develop *Self-Confidence* in relation to situations in which they have experienced positive feedback about the quality of their own performance. →

Learning experiences should be structured in a way that gives all learners the opportunity to succeed at their own current level of functioning.

Learners develop *Self-Acceptance* when they have obtained positive feedback about their own performance in a sufficient variety of personality significant situations. →

All learners should be exposed to as wide as possible a variety of learning strategies, materials and situations.

ALTERNATIVE OPERATIONAL PRACTICES

Appropriately paced *individual learning* with individualized materials, learning mode and feedback.

Homogeneous learning groups with appropriate pace, materials, mode and with individualized feedback.

Heterogeneous grouping with differentiated tasks and/or expectations for learners at different developmental levels and with individualized feedback,

Diversified learning in and out of school using one of previous three operational patterns.

of behaviour which might be mistakenly taken as manifestations
of the construct. An informative discussion of construct definitions with examples is contained in Cronbach (1971). Definitions for these three constructs are also provided in Skager
(1977).

In the first column of the Figure the three constructs
are listed hierarchically on the assumption that they follow
a logical order of development. It seems reasonable to begin at
the point when the learner first becomes aware in an evaluative
sense of his or her own level of functioning. *Self-awareness* is
presumably built on accurate feedback as to how successfully or
unsuccessfully one deals with certain kinds of situation.

In the normal, reality-oriented individual the next construct, *self-confidence*, is assumed to devolve from a generalized awareness that ones' own functioning in a certain class of
situations is adequate. Self-confidence is assumed here to be
situation relevant and based on a generalized history of perceived success in related situations. It is also assumed to be
possible for people to be highly self-confident in some types
of situation and less self-confident in other types of situation, depending on the nature of the feedback they have received from prior experiences.

Finally, it is postulated that a generalized pattern of
self-acceptance develops (or perhaps is maintained since the
very young child may be highly self-confident prior to experi-
encing a situation) in people who have earlier become self-
confident as to their own competencies in a sufficient variety
of situations. In other words, if there are significant areas
of functioning in which an individual feels competent, then
that individual is likely to manifest an overall attitude of
self-acceptance. Since few of us are lucky enough to be successful at everything we are called upon to do, this also implies that it is possible to be generally self-accepting and
at the same time realize that there are some areas in which one
does not function particularly well. The three statements in
the first column form the kernel of a "common sense" theory or
mini-theory about the development of self-concept (2). Each
relates a construct to an educational principle, and the constructs and principles are shown to be interrelated in an admittedly simple, linear way. Since the theory is presented for
illustrative purposes we need not be too concerned if it appears to over-simplify what is a very complex developmental
process.

The second column lists deductions about instructional principles or practices that would presumably contribute to the development of each construct in the theory. Thus, *Self-Awareness* requires accurate feedback to the learner on the quality of his or her performance. Instruction should be designed so as to guarantee that feedback. *Self-Confidence* is in turn based on a history of positive self-perception and facilitated by designing the learning situation so that all learners have the chance to succeed at their own levels of functioning. Finally, *Self-Acceptance* devolves from self-confidence generalized over situations. This principle calls for exposure of the learner to a wide variety of learning strategies, materials and situations, but only under the two prior conditions of accurate feedback and opportunity to succeed. The principles of the theory are thus cumulative and inter-related. The first two constructs are specific to particular classes of situation, while the third (self-acceptance) is stated as a generalized personality characteristic devolving from the other two.

The last step is illustrated by the operational practices listed in the box at the bottom of the Figure. Each of the four practices differ in the mode of learning, but each incorporates the first two instructional principles of accurate feedback and the opportunity for successful performance. The last or "Diversified Learning" paradigm also incorporates the third principle of variety of learning modes. The practices in the box, and others could be listed, are applications derived from the theory. The common-sense theory, then, is useful if it suggests actual operational practices and related evaluation instruments.

The process just described appears to be a promising way of moving from fairly abstract criteria to concrete operational practices. It requires the development or selection of a theory about how people learn, but such theorizing seems inevitable if one is to have a coherent and systematic basis for designing teaching and learning situations. It is also interesting that some of the operational or structural principles of lifelong education enter into this particular example, even though the criteria are derived from the growth cluster referring to characteristics of learners. Thus, the principle of diversification implies horizontal integration, a structural principle. So the approach appears to have the potential for revealing relationships between criteria which refer to structural, organizational or process principles and criteria referring to desired characteristics of learners.

Conclusion

This chapter should above all have made it clear that there are a variety of ways to develop evaluative criteria and that these involve both empirical and theoretical modes of analysis. It should also be evident that the principles of lifelong education are open to interpretation and that the nature of such interpretation is influenced by the cultural context in which it is made. At a relatively general level it is possible for individuals from different countries to agree on criteria for evaluating curricula. The list of combined criteria discussed in this chapter probably illustrates reasonably well the degree of specification that is possible at the multinational level. But in order to develop relevant evaluation instruments and design operational elements of the curriculum it is necessary to go much further in the direction of concrete specification. Two procedures for doing this have been suggested, one involving specification by curriculum component and the other using theory to derive operational practices likely to facilitate various aspects of personal development.

NOTES

1. Factor analysis is a statistical procedure often used to identify patterns in relationship among test or questionnaire items. It identifies items or questions that "go together" in the sense of measuring substantially the same underlying dimensions or factors. Respondents tend to answer such items in the same way. That is, if items i and k have a similar pattern of factor loadings, then an individual who responds with "much emphasis" (one of the response options in the Japanese evaluation study) to item i is likely to respond in the same way to item k. Factors are in the psychological sense constructs which are hypothesized to account for consistencies in the response of individuals to test or questionnaire items.

2. The common-sense theory is obviously based on the idea that the aspects of self-concept referred to are *learned* and also assigned a central role to positive reinforcement in its development. This approach has been taken not out of partisanship but

62   Curriculum Evaluation for Lifelong Education

rather pragmatically because as an illustration the
theory does assign a powerful role to experience and
also readily suggests educational applications.

REFERENCES

Cronbach, L.J. "Test Validation". In Thorndike, R.L.
(ed.). *Educational Measurement*. (2nd ed.). Washington:
American Council on Education, 1971.

Skager, R.W. *Evaluation and Lifelong Education*. Hamburg:
Unesco Institute for Education., 1977.

CHAPTER 5

APPLICATIONS OF THE EVALUATIVE CRITERIA TO VARIOUS ASPECTS OF THE NATIONAL CURRICULA

Overview of National Research Efforts

The purpose of this chapter is one of comparing and contrasting the various approaches selected and used by the three teams in the application of the natinal criterion lists to the evaluation of curricula in their respective countries. There will be no attempt to compare the curricula themselves in terms of relative degree of correspondence to the principles of life-long education. Even if the latter could be done, it is not clear that anything would be gained from the effort. Certainly something would be lost in the standardization across countries of the criteria, instruments for collecting data, and modes of analysis that would be required if meaningful comparisons were to be made. Standardization on a multinational basis would doubtless have reduced the number and variety of approaches explored and perhaps forestalled some of the unique contributions made by specific national teams. From the multinational perspective this research is an exploration of possibilities. National differences in criteria, procedures, and modes of analysis contribute to the number of possibilities explored.

National Samples

The utilization of existing research findings by the Swedish team precluded any need to collect new empirical data from learners, teachers, and parents. The Japanese and Romanian teams on the other hand did have to collect such data and elicited the cooperation of panels of schools for this purpose.

The Japanese selected one elementary, one lower secondary and one upper secondary school for each of four geographic locales: large city suburban, large city inner, rural urbanized, and rural. (The sample was not quite complete in that the inner-city, upper secondary school was missing.) Learners, teachers, and parents from the eleven schools that were included in the panel provided most of the data for the Japanese studies, ex-cept, of course, for the content analysis of the written curri-culum which was based on expert judgment. Most of the learner level data were collected at the 5th grade for the elementary schools (ages 10-11), the 2nd grade of the lower secondary schools (ages 13-14), and the 2nd grade of the upper secondary schools (ages 16-17). The Japanese team did not attempt to ob-tain a representative national sample. Many more schools would have had to be included than was possible given the resources available. Still, the sample was selected so as to provide vari-ation on two common sampling dimensions, urban vs. rural and inner vs. outer city.

The Romanian team followed a similar procedure under si-milar constraints. Four schools participated in the research, providing a total pool of 654 learners, 73 teachers and 432 parents from whom data were successfully collected. Two of the schools were large city, one small town, and one rural. Parents participating in the research represented a wide occupational spectrum, including workers, farmers, intellectuals, office-workers, and housewives. Three of the schools were general schools, with learners sampled at the first and pre-terminal grade for each level, e.g., 1st and 3rd grades for primary, 5th and 7th grades for lower secondary and 9th and 11th for upper secondary (lycée). One of the urban schools was upper secondary only.

Grouping and Comparing National Studies

All of the studies reported here involve the collection and interpretation of empirical data. There are a number of di-mensions on which comparisons between empirical studies can be made, depending on the particular purpose underlying the compar-ison. These include the *source* (teachers, learners, documents, etc.) of data, the *measuring instruments* or *procedures* utilized, the modes of *analysis* applied to the data, as well as the par-ticular *evaluative criteria* addressed in the study. On examina-tion, however, none of these commonly applied comparative dimen-sions appeared to provide a useful approach to grouping the 19 studies (6 Japanese, 6 Swedish, and 7 Romanian) to be surveyed. Many of the national studies, for example, utilize more than one source, often obtaining data from students, teachers, and parents as a part of the same investigation. Classification by source in this case would involve a great deal of repetition in reference to certain studies. The measurement and analysis dimensions on the other hand are technical. They do not provide a means for grouping the studies in terms of substantive characteristics. At first, classification on the basis of evaluative criteria utilized seemed promising. However, it turned out that a number of the studies applied criteria from all five clusters to one or more aspects of the national curriculum. Others applied criteria from two clusters and still others from only one. This again is not a comparison of much interest.

The best approach turned out to be one of grouping the various studies according to the basic purpose or objective of the evaluation. Comparisons will be made among studies that were designed to accomplish something similar. Given this basic comparability of purpose, differences between national studies in procedures, instrumentation and criteria become informative.

There are two fundamentally different approaches to evaluating school curricula. The first is *direct*. It involves analyzing the written curriculum or observing the teaching/learning process. The second is *indirect*. It derives inferences about the quality of the curriculum from observed characteristics of learners who have been exposed to it. It could be argued in favor of the second approach that effects on learners are the only thing that ultimately matters. This is certainly true insofar as all important effects of the school curriculum (intended and unintended) can in fact be determined and separated out from other influences. But the latter is a complex, long-term process. In the shorter term it is quite useful to evaluate aspects of the existing curriculum for congruency with whatever criteria are deemed relevant.

The concept of curriculum presented in Chapter 3 is very broad in scope. In reality it is a concept of multiple curricula rather than of a single school curriculum. This breadth of reference is reflected in the national studies. At the first level, some "direct" studies were concerned solely with the written national curriculum. At a second level studies dealt with extended curriculum operating in the behaviour of teachers and the organization of the school. Implied in this category, of course, is a further distinction between intended and unintended curricula. A third set of studies attempted to assess the nature of the informal curriculum of the family and to some degree the

larger community. None of the studies directly addressed the
self-defined curriculum of the independent learner alluded to
in Chapter 3, although certain aspects of one study were related to this curriculum.

A fourth class of studies were of the "indirect" type,
focussing on characteristics of learners. All of these were
conducted in order to derive inferences about the school curriculum rather than about the other classes of curricula just
mentioned. These studies could be classified with studies in
the second or school level, but will be treated separately for
reasons just discussed. The following categories and sub-categories, then, constitute the basis for grouping the national
studies:

1) The formal or written curriculum

    a) content analyses of curriculum statements
    b) interpretations by various groups of the
       meaning of curriculum statements

2) Curriculum as revealed in the practices and
   policies of schools

    a) teaching practices
    b) other practices and policies

3) Informal curriculum of family and community

    a) reports by parents on what they would
       like schools to accomplish
    b) educational influence of parent on
       learner

4) Curriculum as inferred from the study of learners

    a) reports by learners on own activities
       and proclivities
    b) characteristics of learners revealed in
       observation and other types of assessment.

Each of the four major categories has been further differentiated into two sub-categories. No doubt additional sub-categories would emerge if more studies were done. The above list
is reasonably comprehensive in the light of the definition of
curriculum adopted for the overall research. Certainly the major
categories of curriculum are present with the possible exception
of the "self-learning" curriculum of the independent learners
just alluded to. This latter curriculum was dealt with on at
least one occasion as will be apparent in the discussion of one

of the Romanian studies. However, such a curriculum is implied in category 4a) above whenever the learner is engaged in independent or self-directed learning.

In the presentation of the national studies four categories will form the primary basis for comparison. They constitute the main features of all empirical evaluation studies, and consist of:

1) *Data Sources*, including documents such as the curriculum plan, and education code, teachers, learners, parents, and educational administrators and others;

2) *Instruments and Procedures for Data Collection*, including content analyses of written material, questionnaires, observation, techniques and schedules, rating scales, and interviews;

3) *Procedures for Analyzing Data*, including both qualitative or impressionistic approaches as well as qualitative procedures such as tabulation, statistical tests, and multivariate analytical procedures and other approaches to summarizing data;

4) *Findings and Implications*, summarized for illustrative purposes.

Obviously, so many separate evaluation studies, some of them of major scope, cannot be summarized and contrasted in detail in the space available, nor would such detailed summary be relevant to the purpose of this report. We do intend to give a picture of the ways in which the three national teams went about applying evaluation criteria for lifelong education to their national curricula. Details that entered into the original report such as number and type of subjects, sampling strategies, precise content of questionnaires, research design, descriptions of most data analyses, complete results, qualifications of findings and the like, will often be left out. If a procedure is used in more than one study it need be described only once.

This report also does not scrutinize any of the studies for possible technical flaws or unjustified interpretation as would be the case for a typical review article. The purpose here is strictly one of examining various approaches to the evaluation of curricula according to criteria pertinent to lifelong education.

Evaluations of the Formal or Written Curriculum

Evaluations of the written curriculum were of two types. The Japanese and Swedish teams conducted formal content analyses of written curriculum materials. Both utilized expert judges whose task was to sort elements of the curricula into categories corresponding to the lifelong education criteria. This type of study is quantitative in revealing the degree to which the various criteria are represented in the curriculum. It also seeks consensus through the use of expert judges likely to apply the criteria in a similar fashion.

The second type of evaluation of the written curriculum is represented by a single Swedish study taken from the current literature. This study investigated the ways in which various groups interpreted aspects of the curriculum, in this case goals and objectives. The purpose of this comparative study was one of contrasting the interferences different groups made about the meaning of statements in the written curriculum.

Content Analyses of Statements in the Curriculum

Japan

There is a "course of study" (written curriculum) for each of the three school levels in Japan. Each is divided into four parts:

a) *General Provisions*, including overall guide-lines for the teaching process
b) *Subject-Matter Content*
c) *Moral Education*
d) *Special Activities*, mainly identified with activities of an extra-curricular nature.

The Japanese content analysis concentrated on the General Provisions sections of each of the three curricula. and, for the content areas of Japanese Language, Social Studies and Special Activities, on the Subject-Matter Content sections containing specific instructions for teaching.

Before performing the content analysis the selected parts of the three curricula were divided into "units of analysis" corresponding approximately to single sentences. Some units were considered to have more than one meaning and were sub-divided. Altogether there were 510 units in the study, distributed between General Provisions (83), Social Studies (184), Japanese (156) and Special Activities (87). These basic elements were analyzed separately by curriculum category.

In the previous chapter we reported that the list of criteria developed by the Japanese team was stated at a considerably more general level than was the case for the other two national teams. The Japanese criteria subsumed sub-categories of
the five major clusters cited in Chapter 4 and paraphrased here
as: Attitude to Self-Learning (ASL), Learning Skills (LS),
Flexible Teaching (FT), Horizontal Integration (HI), Vertical
Articulation (VA), plus a Miscellaneous cluster (M). The latter,
at least for the Subject-Matter Content analyses, contained
mostly statements relating to

a) learning materials and activities pertinent
   to a particular content area; and

b) fairly specific rules about the kinds of content that ought to be emphasized.

Both of these latter sub-categories were characterized in the
Japanese report as restrictions imposed on teaching by the
curriculum writers. Such restrictions were seen to be in potential conflict with the principles of lifelong education expressed in the ASL criteria (opportunity for developing skills
in independent learning) as well as in the FT criteria (flexibility of teaching in the interest of individualization).

The question of how much flexibility had been built into
the curriculum was the central concern of the content analysis
conducted by the Japanese. Their report (in all cases we refer
to the English language version) suggests that criticism has
been voiced within Japanese educational circles to the effect
that the national curriculum might be significantly less flexible than the curricula of a number of other developed countries. In light of this criticism the Japanese team was particularly interested in determining the relative proportions of
curriculum units falling into categories ASL and FT (indicating
flexibility) as compared to those falling into category M (indicating lack of flexibility). The illustration of the Japanese
findings given in Table 5.1 bears directly on this issue. In
the table (adopted from the English version of the Japanese report, p.27) the numerals refer to the number of units of the
social studies curriculum classified under each criterium cluster, broken down by school level. (See next page.)

A comparison of the two "flexibility" categories (ASL
plus FT) with the miscellaneous category (M) shows that in this

particular case the number of statements indicating flexibility
amounts to 54 or about 29% of the total of 184 units, while the
number of units associated with lack of flexibility is 58 or a-
bout 30% of the total. Overall the analysis of the social studies curriculum presents the least favourable picture in all of
the Japanese findings. Content analyses of the other portions
of the school curricula showed a greater preponderance of units
classified under one of the two flexibility categories. Although
the authors of the Japanese report were cautious in drawing inferences, they did conclude that the written curriculum contained many of the necessary elements for moving towards the im-
plementations of lifelong educational principles.

TABLE 5.1

RESULTS OF CONTENT ANALYSIS OF JAPANESE SOCIAL
STUDIES CURRICULUM BROKEN DOWN BY SCHOOL LEVEL

Criterion Category	ASL	LS	FT	HI	VA	M
Elementary	0	1	9	6	3	10
L. Secondary	0	13	20	12	3	22
U. Secondary	10	8	15	22	4	26

The English language version of the full Japanese report
concentrated more on findings than on procedures. However, it
should be pointed out that the content analysis was conducted
by a single judge. During the development of the Swedish criteria (described in Chapter 4) two judges conducted independent
trial content analyses, making it possible to assess the extent
to which there was consistency of judgment.

Sweden

The Swedish criterion list utilized five major categories
cited in the previous chapter: Horizontal Integration (HI),
Vertical Integration (VI), Individual Maturity and Self-Realization (MSR), Autodidactics (A) and Creativity, Flexibility and

Equality (CFE). These categories were broken down into two additional levels of specificity ("Sub-Categories" and "Definitions"), leading to considerably more statements (81 in 26 sub-
categories) than in the case of the Japanese list.

The Swedish content analysis concentrated on three parts
of the national curriculum:

1) the general part including goals, guidelines
   and general directives of the basic school
   curriculum (LGR 69);

2) the same or general part of the upper secondary school curriculum (LGR 70);

3) a set of basic guidelines or proposals developed by a committee on the international work
   of the school (coded SIA in the Swedish report),
   established in 1970 by a directive of the national parliament. This committee's task was
   to recommend improvements in the climate of the
   school from the point of view of the student.

It will be recalled that these three portions of the curriculum were broken down into small "units" consisting of sentences or sentence fragments ultimately reproduced individually
on cards. In the content analysis two judges sorted the unit
cards into one or more of the 26 sub-criteria. The judges worked
together in this process, since the degree of agreement between
the judges working separately had already been assessed during
the pilot phase of the study. Units classified under more than
one sub-criterion obviously incorporated more than one principle of lifelong education. In no case, however, were units classified under more than one sub-criterion within the same criterion cluster.

The Swedish report utilizes several interesting approaches
in reporting the content analyses. However, it was first necessary to establish comparability in the metric by which results
were reported from curriculum to curriculum and from analysis
to analysis. Since the Swedish team wanted to compare sections
of curricula in terms of the extent to which they incorporated
principles of lifelong education, mere frequencies would have
been misleading in being biased by the varying lengths of the
curriculum sections. Thus, a high frequency of units consistent
with lifelong education criteria might indicate only that a particular curriculum section was longer than other sections. In

addition, the Swedish team wished to determine the relative frequency of units consistent with the criteria to the total number of units contained in a given section. This analysis also required comparability from section to section. This desired comparability was achieved by converting the lengths of all units and texts to the same standard, as described below. While examples of all the analyses cannot be given, the ways in which the problems were dealt with deserve illustration here, as the procedures are applicable to any written curriculum.

The Swedish report proceeded from the general to the specific. First, for each of the three curricula an overall breakdown was provided on the extent to which each of the five criterion clusters was represented in each of the three curricula. An example from the secondary level curriculum is given in Table 5.2 (Box 2 of the Swedish report, p.37)

TABLE 5.2

EXTENT OF OCCURRENCE OF MAIN CRITERIA IN CURRICULUM
FOR UPPER SECONDARY SCHOOL (Lgy 70)

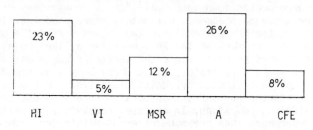

HI = Horizontal Integration
VI = Vertical Integration
MSR = Individual Maturity and Self-Realization
A   = Autodidactics
CFE = Creativity, Flexibility, Equality

Table 5.2 and similar tables for the two other curricula are mutually comparable because the lengths of all units and texts were converted to the same standard. This was done by

    a) computing the average number of words included
       in one line of the basic school curriculum (Lgy 69)

b) standardizing all units as well as the original
texts by dividing the total number of words by
this average.

Table 5.2 shows that the HI and A criterion categories each account for about one fourth of the units of the upper secondary
curriculum. Two of the other criterion categories are not so
well represented, however, Tables not reproduced here showed a
similar relative emphasis on HI and A. One difference between
curricula noted in the Swedish report is the greater emphasis
on criterion category VI in the SIA curriculum (recommendations
of the parliamentary panel on school climate).

It should be recognized that the comparisons in Table 5.2
and those that follow refer solely to the frequency of units
consistent with particular criteria. The frequencies do not reflect the *importance* or *weight* of individual units. Thus a single statement in a cluster or sub-criterion with low frequency
for a given curriculum might imply more in terms of impact on
the teaching/learning process than ten statements from a cluster or sub-criterion of high frequency. Still, the tables as a
whole probably reflect fairly accurately the relative emphasis
given to the various criteria in the curricula analyzed.

Table 5.3 (Box 5 of the Swedish report, p.39) shows a different type of summary analysis, this one breaking the curricula down into sections and showing the proportion of "lines"
(unit length converted to standard scale) consistent with the
criteria as compared to the total number of lines per section.
(See next page.) The standardization procedures also reveal the
relative emphasis given to each curriculum section. The Swedish
team concluded for the upper secondary curriculum that the written curriculum, with the exception of the section on information
about students (including evaluation of work), is reasonably
consistent with the lifelong education criteria.

A third type of analysis at a still more specific level
is illustrated in Table 5.4 (taken from Box 8, p.48). Here the
sub-criteria for the first of the five major criterion categories (HI) were analyzed separately. (Brief labels for each sub-
criterion are given in the Table.) The Swedish team repeated
this analysis for the rest of the five criterion categories.

The summary data of Table 5.4 (see p. 75) show the relative emphasis given to various sub-criteria of the HI category.
It is difficult to establish, admittedly, how much of a sub-

criterion is "good". That is, what is the most desirable frequency of representation for a given sub-criterion in a given curriculum. On the other hand, relative emphasis among sub-categories is established, and it is readily apparent in this particular example that certain sub-categories are given little if any emphasis, while others are reflected in many units.

TABLE 5.3

THE PROPORTION OF UNITS ON LIFELONG LEARNING IN DIFFERENT SECTIONS OF THE CURRICULUM FOR THE UPPER SECONDARY SCHOOL (Lgy 70)

Number of Lgr lines
in each section

Number of Lgr lines
favourable to life-
long learning

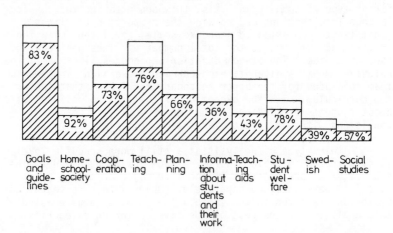

TABLE 5.4

NUMBER OF LINES FAVOURABLE TO LIFELONG LEARNING BELONGING
TO THE MAIN CRITERIA A [HI in this report] DIVIDED BETWEEN
SUB-CATEGORIES, EXPRESSED IN A PERCENTAGE OF THE TOTAL
NUMBER OF LINES IN THE CURRICULUM FOR THE UPPER SECONDARY
SCHOOL (Lgy 70)

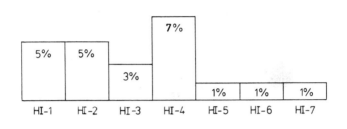

HI-1 = School - home
HI-2 = School - society
HI-3 = School - working life
HI-4 = School - subjects
HI-5 = School - mass media
HI-6 = School - cultural life
HI-7 = Implementation (suggested measures for application)

One other type of analysis was conducted for each criterion category and is illustrated with an example in Table 5.5,
(see next page). This analysis provides for each of the three
curricula a breakdown of the proportion of lines devoted to the
sub-categories of each criterion category by curriculum section.
For example, Table 5.5 shows that 7% of the lines in the "Goals
and Guidelines" section of the Lgy 70 curriculum referred to integration of home and school. This type of analysis seems to be
a potentially useful analytical tool for determining the relative weight given to specific criteria in various sections of
a written curriculum.

The Swedish team drew a great number of specific conclusions from their very detailed analysis. They noted, for example,

TABLE 5.5
PROPORTION OF THE RESPECTIVE SWEDISH CURRICULUM SECTIONS,
EXPRESSED IN PERCENTAGES, THAT DEAL WITH THE SUB-CRITERIA
HI-1 TO HI-7 [A 1 TO A 7 BELOW] FOR CURRICULUM Lgy 70

Part-criteria⎯Section	A 1 Home	A 2 Society	A 3 Working life	A 4 School-subjects	A 5 Mass media	A 6 Cultural life	A 7 Implementation	Total %
Goals and guidelines	7	10	4	2		1	1	25
Home-school-society	44	23	3		6			76
Cooperation	3	8	11	3				25
Teaching		3	4	15				22
Planning	1	1	2	37	1	2		44
Evaluation	0			0			3	3
Teaching aids			1		1	4		6
Student welfare	18	5	1					24
Swedish								
Social studies		52						52

that the important sub-criterion of self-evaluation was very poorly covered. Overall, however, they found the existing curricula to be reasonably compatible with the lifelong education criteria. Their report also took care to recognize that excellence of a written curriculum does not necessarily guarantee that the principles involved will be implemented adequately in programmes of the school. The reminder of the Swedish report scrutinised this issue through the existing research literature.

Summary

Taken together, the three national reports present an interesting contrast in terms of the utilization of content analysis procedures. The Romanian team decided not to conduct such an analysis and directed their efforts in quite different directions. The Japanese team did conduct a content analysis, but devoted only moderate resources to the effort. The Swedish team, in contrast, confined their empirical work entirely to this type of analysis and as a result provided a very detailed illustration of the kinds of procedure that may be used and findings that may accrue.

Interpretation of the Meaning of Statements in the Curriculum

The Swedish report summarizes research by Stencrantz, et al., (1973) that utilized an approach other than content analysis for written curricula. This work was undertaken to determine the quality of a curriculum in terms of the kinds of interpretation people make of its contents.

The Goals and Directives section of the Lgr 69 basic school curriculum was first examined by the research group. Eight general goal areas were found to be represented. (The authors of the Swedish report for the present study noted that seven out of the eight goals corresponded to sub-criteria of the third, or MSR cluster, of their criterion list.) Next, nineteen different groups, each with about seven members, were given definitions of the goals plus relevant sections of the Lgr 69 curriculum. The groups included teachers, members of political parties and labour unions, parents, employers, and students. Participants were asked to read the relevant materials and then to interpret the meaning of each goal area in terms of their personal perceptions of the intentions of the curriculum writers. The responses were ultimately grouped by the researchers into six main categories.

The results revealed that the goals inferred by the researchers differed from the interpretation made by the various participating groups. There was considerably less emphasis on MSR type criteria for the latter. This finding suggests that the curriculum was not written at a level concrete enough to ensure that various groups would interpret its statements in approximately the same way. The authors of the Swedish report suggest that without concrete examples teachers will find it difficult to translate the principles embodied in the curriculum into the teaching/learning process.

Implications

The Stencrantz, et al., (1973) study appears to offer a useful approach to evaluating a written curriculum in terms of its actual meaning to both lay and professional readers. It is a relatively non-technical approach that has the advantage of including representative elements of the whole society in addition to the usual curriculum experts.

Curriculum as Revealed in School Practices and Policies

By far the largest group of evaluative studies in the national reports deals in one way or another with the curriculum as it is manifest in the schools. A number of these studies concentrates on teaching, and these will be treated separately, although distinctions are not always easy to make between practices associated solely with teaching and other influences.

Evaluating Teaching Practices

There are of course many approaches to evaluating teaching practices. Some are direct in that they involve actual observation of the instructional process. Others are indirect and require inferences about how teachers would be likely to behave. Examples of the latter would include

a) asking teachers about their teaching methods;

b) eliciting beliefs and attitudes from teachers that might be expected to influence their teaching.

The national teams conducted studies which fall into both categories.

Japan

By polling teachers from the sample of *schools described*

above (plus one special sample to be described later) the Japanese team surveyed several dimensions of teacher attitudes and opinions that would presumably have a bearing on the implementation of lifelong education. This was done by means of questionnaire items and included coverage of the following topics:

a) attitudes to lifelong education itself;

b) school goals rated in terms of importance to lifelong education;

c) opinions about extent to which students should be allowed to select their own programme of studies;

d) amount of emphasis reported by teachers on activities hypothesized to enhance learner educability;

e) latent curriculum as manifested in the patterns of evaluation preferred by the teachers.

While it is not possible here to cover all of the findings, illustrations can be provided. For general aspects of a) above virtually all teachers had either heard of or were to some extent familiar with the phrase "lifelong education". About 64% reported that they had at least thought about school education from that perspective. The teachers were also asked in a questionnaire to rate each of 13 educational objectives considered to contribute to lifelong education for both "attainability" and "necessity" (importance). In abstracted form, 13 goals were:

1) development of a realistic self-concept;

2) understanding of adult (post-school) social roles;

3) preparation for living in a changing society;

4) ability and motivation toward good citizenship;

5) critical thinking ability;

6) ability to evaluate;

7) development of skills and motivation for continued independent learning;

8) development of a sense of moral responsibility;

9) ability to use leisure effectively;

10) problem-solving ability;

11) ability to define or be aware of problems;

12) development of a perspective on a personal life role;

13) defining one's position within the history of mankind.

Results showed that the total sample of teachers saw the goals as necessary or important, but at least some were scep- tical about the attainability of several goals, especially 2), 3), 9), 12) and 13). Goals considered to be particularly im- portant such as 7) dealing with independent learning and 8) with moral responsibility were mainly seen as "attainable to only a certain extent". So overall, there is strong sympathy among teachers with the goals formulated by the Japanese team, but a tendency to question whether all can be fully implemented. The statements were phrased at a very general level. One would expect a high degree of acquiescence among respondents in such cases, but there still were differentiations between goal state- ments, especially in the ratings of attainability. These de- ferences may pinpoint areas of resistance among teachers.

The teachers also responded to questions specifically di- rected at characteristics of schooling within the perspective of lifelong education, as implied in b) above. In this area teachers saw self-learning (educability), cooperation with home and cooperation with community as especially important school goals. Oddly enough, they rated "developing interests of students in learning" relatively low, although this would appear to be closely related to self-learning.

Because the Japanese curriculum allows relatively little choice on the part of students among courses or subjects of study (none at all in elementary and lower secondary and only in the case of a few subjects in upper secondary), the response to questions about student choice in c) are especially interesting. Here there seems to be some, but by no means overwhelming, sup- port for giving more choice to learners, with an overall pro- portion of about 40% in favour at all levels and about 50% at the upper secondary level. Some of the findings in d), pertain- ing to preferred educational activities, are closely related. Although the approach to enhancing learner educability by far most favoured by teachers was "independent thinking and discov- ery", a presumably related class of activities involving the development of "skills in planning, conducting and evaluating their new studies" was rated quite low. While an interpretation of this interesting inconsistency was not advanced in the Japanese report, it may be that many of the teachers saw their own role in the management of the classroom as potentially less important if so much responsibility were to be assigned to students.

The Japanese team in addition conducted a separate questionnaire study on a special sample of teachers in a small city several hours by train from the heavily urbanized Tokyo area. The city was deemed to be in a transition point with respect to modernization. The questionnaire listed some 30 categories of teaching content, all but three of which were suggested by a panel of curriculum specialists as potentially controversial. The 300 plus teachers in the special sample were asked to rate each content category in terms of its suitability for compulsory education. Generally, the Japanese team reported signs of a considerable degree of liberalization among these teachers as evidenced by their willingness to teach topics implying integration between school content and society, such as current social issues.

Two additional Japanese studies dealt with activities that are not usually thought of as teaching *per se*, but which are nevertheless an important part of the teacher's job. The first of these studies surveyed the patterns by which teachers evaluated learners. The second dealt with principles emphasized in the guidance of learners. Both the evaluation and the guidance functions were identified in the Japanese report with the "latent" curriculum of the school, or that part of the curriculum that is independent of subject-matter content and at least in part unplanned in the formal sense.

The evaluation study was based on 14 questionnaire items administered to all teachers in the regular sample of 11 schools. Seven of the items described modes of evaluation such as published tests, teacher constructed essay or objective tests, etc. The remaining items asked about factors external to the school having an influence on the teacher as a curriculum planner. These included textbooks, entrance examinations, and requirements at later grade levels. Teachers responded by indicating the extent to which they emphasized each factor. The resulting data were submitted to a principle components factor extraction procedure followed by varimax rotation (2). Four factors were extracted and interpreted as revealing the following basic orientations to the evaluation of learners:

Factor 1: This factor incorporated patterns of evaluation emphasizing the use of examinations. The item with the highest loading (.756) was "essay tests of teacher's own making".

Factor 2: This factor combines evaluation modes that take into account the conditions of learning and characteristics of the learners. Items with the highest loadings were "the actual conditions of a community" (.755) and "learning attitudes in class" (.724).

Factor 3: This factor is really not interpretable except in a negative sense. The only item with a non-trivial positive loading was "other methods of evaluation" (.674). Most items had near zero or low negative loadings, except for "the contents considered necessary after leaving school" (-.544). In other words, teachers who said they used methods of evaluation not on the list tended to respond inconsistently to all but one of the other items.

Factor 4: The fourth factor is identified primarily with the curriculum planning items and reflects an emphasis on the official curriculum as implied in "the official course of study" (.727) and "textbooks" (.723). Also related are "entrance examinations or examinations for employment" (.6) and "the contents considered necessary at a higher grade" (.522).

The four basic evaluation and planning patterns in part characterize different levels of schooling. This was revealed when average factor scores were calculated for each of the 11 schools in the sample (3). Upper secondary and to some extent lower secondary schools emphasized the first or "examinations" factor. Not surprisingly, elementary schools had high factor scores on the second or "conditions of learning" factor. For reasons that are not entirely clear, lower secondary schools had the highest factor scores on the remaining two factors. The Japanese report concluded that the emphasis on preparation for entrance examinations, evident especially at the upper secondary level, could constitute a negative climate for the development of a "sound attitude toward self-learning" as well as "encouragement of flexible teaching".

The guidance study also used factor analytic procedures, but need be mentioned only briefly as the use of such procedures was illustrated in the study just discussed. This final study of the teaching process conducted by the Japanese team devolved from the same questionnaire. Teachers indicated the degree of emphasis they placed on each of 21 themes in their guidance of the daily activities of learners. These included physical health, perseverence, tidiness, being cooperative in group activities, etc.

The factor analysis yielded three factors corresponding roughly to an emphasis on positive *moral and social values* (Factor 1), emphasis on *desirable behaviour patterns and etiquette* (Factor 2), and maintaining a *sense of responsibility to others* (Factor 3). There was no clear-cut preference at the upper secondary level, but the lower secondary teachers had the highest scores on the second factor and the elementary teachers the highest loadings on the third factor.

Romania

The Romanian team also conducted an intensive study of teachers in the sample described earlier, utilizing questionnaires, direct observation and interviews. The study had purposes rather similar to those of the Japanese work just described, especially in emphasizing teachers' preferences about goals, activities and subject-matter content in the perspective of lifelong education. This similarity is apparent in the following selection of topics abstracted from the questionnaire:

a) importance attached to various principles of lifelong education;

b) relative desirability of various mechanisms for achieving integration of school and world of work, community, family, etc.

c) relative desirability of various teaching methods and processes from the perspective of the teacher;

d) attempts by teacher to organize subject matter in a way that integrates disciplines;

e) relative importance of various pupil characteristics relating to growth and educability;

f) criteria used by the teacher in evaluating
students;

g) relevant criteria for selecting optional
courses and subjects;

h) suggestions about possible additions to curriculum consistent with lifelong education.

The findings obtained from the teacher questionnaire were
given considerable emphasis in the Romanian report. Although
the criterion list developed by the Romanian team was the most
detailed and comprehensive of the three, the criteria dealing
with relationships between school and society were held to be
of special importance within the national context. Illustrative
findings in this area relating to integration of the school and
the world of work included the fact that teachers placed greatest emphasis on developing work-related curiosity and generalized technical skills and interests directly through school subjects. Pure vocational training of a general nature ranked second, while organization of productive school units through con-
tracts with state enterprises and creation of school workshops
staffed by students and workers ranked low. About 20% of the
teachers still favoured the latter option, however. The teachers'
preferences for facilitating the development of general skills
is consistent with the emphasis in lifelong edcuation on traits
related to educability. In the area of integration between school
and family the responses of the teachers reveal a preference for
direct, rather than indirect, modes of contact.

As to preferred modes of teaching, both the questionnaire
study and the ratings of related criteria showed the teachers to
be interested in applying discovery approaches to learning. This
is again consistent with the emphasis on educability or self-
learning found in lifelong education. However, the questionnaire
revealed that the most commonly used teaching method was lessons
accompanied by questions from students.

Finally, the learner evaluation criteria preferred by
teachers included logical and creative thinking, ability to apply learning, and evidence of ability to learn independently.
Exact recall of what had been taught was placed last.

A second type of study conducted by the Romanian team uti-

lized a mainly qualitative approach. It investigated individualization of learning beginning with the first year of school and
extending into the secondary school. Interviews of teaching
staff and informal observation of the activities of learners
in the classroom were conducted. The information thus obtained
was summarized in the national report by means of descriptions
of individualized learning activities at various school levels.
The Romanian team found considerable evidence to the effect
that learners were acting independently in a variety of ways
to the school context.

Sweden

Three of the studies identified in the literature by the
Swedish team dealt with teaching practices. The first two were
the products of a long-term project analyzing the teaching process into its main components ("Didactic Process Analysis").
The authors of the Swedish report were especially interested
in this work of Bredänge, et. al. (1971 and 1972) for the light
that it might shed on the kinds of practice teachers utilize to
promote self-learning or "autodidactics", as the category is
labelled in the Swedish list.

The work was based on lengthy videotape recordings of 80
teachers and their classes, the latter divided into 60 regular
classes and 20 classes for children with various types of handi-
cap. Ten lessons were recorded for each class and systematic a-
nalyses of the behaviour of students and teachers were conducted by means of ratings and formal observation schedules. In the
latter, teacher and student behaviours were recorded by six observers working independently. The level of agreement among the
observers was reported to be about equal to the reliability expected of the typical published objective test. An example of
one category of behaviours on the teacher observation schedule
is:

> "Encourages students to draw their own conclusions.
> Presents the students with a problem and tells
> them to find different ways of solving it (learn-
> ing by discovery) " (p.116).

While viewing the videotapes the observers recorded how
often instances of each category of behaviour occurred. When
totalled for each teacher these frequencies provided a profile
of individual performance. Total frequencies over the approximately 600 observations of the 60 teachers constituted a group
profile.

The overall profile for the entire sample did not give an encouraging picture from the point of view of lifelong education. Teacher behaviours that might contribute to the development of autonomy in learners (like the one quoted above) were relatively infrequent as compared to behaviours in which the learners played dependent roles. The original authors reported that most of the teaching was of the "whole class" variety with the teacher lecturing and the learners passively receiving. Factual knowledge was heavily stressed. Students were required to reproduce concrete facts, descriptions and accounts.

The second study in the project by Bredänge and Odhagen (1972) delved more deeply into the data. Latent profile analysis was used to isolate five groups of teachers with similar behavioural profiles. The largest of these groups (26 out of the 59 teachers in this particular analysis) displayed a profile almost identical to the average profile for the group as a whole. In contrast two of the groups showed patterns consistent with one or more sub-criteria in the autodidactic category. The descriptions are quoted here from the Swedish national report:

> "Group 2 (nine teachers). Student-centering is characteristic of the group. Behaviours noted here are "ego-strengthening", such as strong positive feedback and alertness to students' opinions, interests and experiences."

> "Group 5 (seven teachers). The most noticeable feature in this group is that it gets the students to work with different activities at the same time and that the teacher moves around among the students, giving individual instruction and group teaching. The teacher behaviour in the teaching process is characterized by a high degree of student activity and by individual guidance from the teacher " (p.118).

The Swedish team concluded that these two groups of teachers appeared to be preparing students for autonomous-learning. Specific aspects of the above statements were shown to be consistent with various sub-criteria of the Swedish autodidactic category. The fact that at least some teachers out of the total sample did demonstrate patterns of behaviour consistent with what the Swedish team considered "the most central concept" in lifelong education was taken as a hopeful sign. The potentialities of systematic observation coupled with latent structure analyses for going deeper than is possible with overall summary data were cited in the Swedish report.

The third study by the Swedish team searched for relationships between observed teacher behaviours and creativity in learners. As a part of a larger study Eriksson (1972) related systematic observations of teachers in 23 sixth grade classrooms to performance of learners on tests of creativity. Observed teacher behaviours were classified in one of four categories, depending on the type of "thought process" they appeared to encourage in students:

1) *Reproductive*, or emphasis on rote learning and memorization;

2) *Convergent*, or emphasis on norms for behaviour and obtaining the single correct solution;

3) *Divergent*, or emphasis on obtaining own facts and producing several solutions, and

4) *Assessment*, or emphasis on critical evaluation, and weighing of evidence in arriving at a personal opinion.

In this study little or no relationship could be found between tested learner creativity and the kinds of thought processes encouraged by teachers since the great majority of the teacher behaviours were classified in the first two categories (66 and 25 percent, respectively). Slightly less than 10% of the recorded behaviours of teachers were in the divergent or assessment mode. While the results might be disappointing, the Eriksson study is especially interesting from the perspective of method. Teacher behaviours hypothesized to be related to a sub-category (creativity) of the CFE-cluster of the Swedish list were defined concretely enough to be observed systematically and in turn related to objective measures of learner performance. Research which correlates teacher behaviour with characteristics observed in learners has a much stronger potential for generating causal relationships than does the study of either class of variables alone.

Other School Practices

The classroom behaviour of teachers is usually thought of as the most patent factor in the overall impact of the school. However, other events and processes are also characteristic of schooling, and the Swedish report surveys one

study dealing with these factors. Axelsson and Ekman (1973) surveyed 104 schools chosen randomly on a national basis. Their
study focussed on relations between school and home as well as
on how schools at different levels exchanged information about
matriculating students. The study is pertinent to criterion categories HI and VI of the Swedish list. A questionnaire was distributed to school principals, teachers, student welfare personnel and representatives of parent organizations.

With respect to integration between school and home, the
study revealed that some parents had little if any contact with
the school. The most important contribution of this aspect of
the study was a set of suggestions about strategies for improving contact between home and school as abstracted from questionnaire responses from members of parental organizations.

The larger study of articulation of students from lower
to upper levels of the school revealed the modes by which information from one level to the other was exchanged as well as
the kinds of information exchanged. Gaps and problems in this
process were noted. Some concern was expressed by respondents
about the propriety of putting middle level teachers' subjective
personal evaluations of students into the permanent written record. It was also learned that information needed at the beginning of the year relating to student illnesses or disabilities
was often not available at that time. Probably the major conclusion of the study was that teachers, who are in a position
to be most familiar with individual students, should engage to
a greater extent in the type of student welfare work usually
left to specialized professionals such as psychologists and
counsellors. The most salient methodological feature of the
Axelsson and Ekman study was the way in which the views and experiences of various groups were combined to give a more accurate picture of educational processes than any single group
might have contributed alone.

Summary of Studies of Operational Curricula

Evaluation studies of the operating school curriculum conducted or reviewed by the three national teams concentrated
mainly on teaching practices. The latter incorporates virtually
all of the intended curriculum in most schools and doubtless a
good deal of the so-called "hidden" curriculum. Within this
broad category of teaching practice there was great variation
in questions asked and methods employed.

One approach was illustrated in the Romanian study which presented teachers with the evaluation criteria developed for the study and asked them, by means of interviews and question- naires, to indicate the relative importance of each. The Japa- nese did something very similar and in addition obtained ratings from teachers on

a) the importance of various activities and ob- jectives within the lifelong education frame- work,

b) the relevance of various types of subject- matter content, and

c) the emphasis given by teachers to various modes of evaluation and principles of guidance (latent curriculum).

A second Romanian study parallels the later Japanese work by surveying teachers on their practices. This first group of studies was based entirely on self-reports by teachers. This is a direct and efficient approach to obtaining information. How- ever, in drawing conclusions it should always be recalled that the actual behaviour of respondents may differ significantly from their stated beliefs and preferences.

A second approach used in the national studies has the advantage of being based on objective observations of teacher behaviour. It has the concomitant disadvantage of involving costlier, more time-consuming procedures for data collection. Reliability and validity of the data are also concerns. Several of the studies reviewed by the Swedish team were of this variety, utilizing formal observations of the teaching process. Such ob- servations, of course, must be structured around hypotheses de- rived from theory or other conceptualization as to the kinds of teacher behaviour that are desirable or undesirable.

There are two avenues to the generation of data on teacher behaviour. The first utilizes ratings by expert or trained judges on one or more behavioural dimensions defined by the re- searcher. The second is much more elaborate, requiring that the frequency of various specific types of behaviour be systemati- cally recorded over a definite interval of time. Unlike the rating method, value judgments about desirability are not made at the time the data are collected. These two approaches have been referred to as *high-* and *low-inference*, respectively, in the book on the evaluation of teaching by Rosenshine and Furst (1971). The observation schedules of the studies reviewed in the Swedish report were of the latter type.

The final type of evaluation study combines two of the major categories under which the various studies are grouped in this report. The last of the Swedish studies reviewed attempted to relate observed teacher behaviours to presumably related outcomes in learners. This is the most costly and complex approach of all, but is also the only one with a potential for identifying causal relationships.

Finally, it is vitally important in research on the teaching process that multiple approaches be utilized for the collection of data, as was the case for several of the studies just summarized. This is equally true for the studies remaining to be discussed. It is always better to have both self-reports by teachers and observations by expert judges than either method taken alone. If two approaches to measuring the same phenomena converge, i.e. yield the same conclusions, then greater confidence can be placed in the results.

Informal Curriculum of Family and Community

Averch, et al., (1972) in a comprehensive review of research on the effectiveness of schooling found considerable evidence suggesting that differences in the achievement of learners are more closely related to non-school factors such as home environment than they are to variables associated with schooling. While this generalization is still a controversial one, there is no denying the fact that a powerful informal curriculum exists in the home, the peer group, and the wider community. Two of the national studies were directly concerned with parental influence in this curriculum.

Parental Views of What Schools Should Accomplish
An indirect way of assessing the nature of parental influence is to ask parents what they think schools should accomplish. The reasoning here is presumably that parents will strive to exert the same kind of influence in their own educational role. If parents are generally sympathetic to a set of educational principles, the home environment probably reflects those principles, to some degree. However, in most societies the attitudes of parents as a group place limits on what schools can attempt to accomplish. A particularly interesting type of evaluation therefore involves an assessment of the extent to which

parents in a given society are sympathetic to the principles of lifelong education.

Japan

The Japanese team administered an extensive questionnaire to mothers of 5th, 8th and 11th grade children in the regular sample of schools. Responses were received from 770 elementary, 1832 lower secondary, and 952 upper secondary mothers. Items on the questionnaire were in part derived from the lifelong education criteria, but also reflected general concerns that might exist in the minds of parents.

Probably the most striking finding of this Japanese survey study was the evidence for an intense parental preoccupation with academic degrees. Leaving out the village schools, about 30% of the parents aspired to graduate education for their sons. (Rather significant differences existed between level of parental aspirations for sons and daughters.) The Japanese report noted that there appeared to be a marked ambivalence in parental views. On the one hand parents were found to be quite idealistic about the traits their children would display as adults. For example, consideration for others and the ability to work cooperatively with others were highly stressed. In contrast, the emphasis on obtaining academic degrees could easily generate strongly competitive attitudes in learners, and within the Japanese context especially in males. The Japanese report expressed concern that this factor plus the tendency to identify education solely with formal degree programmes could create a home atmosphere incompatible with several principles of lifelong education.

The Japanese report contains a variety of findings relating to differences between parental attitudes for different levels of schooling and different regional contexts. Of these probably the most important bear on parental attitudes toward individualization of instruction. Overall, only about 22% favoured individualization, and the greater proportion of these parents hoped that their children would obtain at least an undergraduate education. Approximately 32% rated individualization as undesirable and 45% simply did not know. Since individualization is a central principle in the criterion cluster corresponding to self-learning, this finding also suggests that current parental attitudes are not entirely supportive of principles of lifelong education.

Other questions assessed attitudes toward additional formal education outside of the regular school (a common practice in Japan, especially among parents with high educational aspirations for their children), as well as attitudes toward extracurricular cultural and physical training. Finally, an interesting set of questions already alluded to probed parental aspirations as to the personal characteristics of their children as adults. Items consisted of brief descriptions of adult characteristics such as, a person wishes "to lead a comfortable life" (rated lowest with only about 9% rating it desirable) or, a person who "can continue efforts to solve his or her own problems" (rated highest at 77%). Overall, the responses of parents stress the model adult as actively working, cooperative with others, moderate in personal life and integrated in personality. This pattern, while implying a degree of ambivalence when juxtaposed with information about academic aspirations, does reflect an idealism compatible with lifelong education.

Romania

The Romanian team also administered a questionnaire to parents, part of which assessed parental views about the objectives of school education. Their study dealt in addition with the education of children in the family, cooperation between the home and the school, and parental preferences as to the criteria the school should use in evaluating learners.

Some 432 parents with children in the 1st, 3rd, 5th, 7th, 9th and 11th grades participated in the study. The Romanian team concluded that several factors in the attitudes of parents suggested a favourable climate for the introduction of lifelong education into the schools, while at least one other did not. Among the former was the primary emphasis parents placed on preparation for productive work, on helping the child to learn to integrate the self according to ideals, and to improving the teaching process to facilitate achievement on the part of learners. On the other side was the relative lack of concern on the part of parents with the potential role of the school in teaching children how to learn (e.g., self-learning), although support for this function was higher among urban parents.

Another type of question which was posed to parents by the Romanian team assessed the impact of the school on parents themselves. Virtually all parents agree that they had learnt from their own contact with their children's schools. Ranked first were knowledge about child rearing and their own role in educating children. Also important were revisions of ideas about school and society as well as content knowledge in some new field. These findings suggest that a considerable degree of horizontal integration between home and school already exists in the eyes of the parents.

Finally, parents were asked about their reactions to the process by which the school evaluated their children. Ranked first as a criterion among parents was motivation to work and personal effort expended. Ability to apply what had been learnt came second. The mere desire to obtain good marks was seen as the least important of the alternatives offered. These findings are also compatible with principles of lifelong education.

Educational Influence of Parent

The direct educational influence of the parent on the child is both a very large as well as a very subtle area of inquiry. All but one of the national studies assigned priorities to other types of data. Fortunately, it was at least touched on in the Romanian questionnaire study just discussed. Parents were asked about the kind of thing stressed within the family, using the following categories:

a) independence and sense of responsibility,

b) work and the appreciation of work,

c) obedience and discipline,

d) finding own way in life,

e) curiosity, interest in new things and creativity,

f) love of books, culture and learning.

The findings revealed greatest emphasis on work and love of work followed by appreciation of books and culture. Lowest ranked were a) and e) above reflecting an emphasis on independence and creativity.

Summary of Studies of Parents

Two of the three multi-national studies devoted some effort to assessing influences of the home that directly affect the education of the child or that indicate the kind of attitudinal climate that exists with respect to pertinent educational principles. The two national teams that assessed parental attitudes found both positive and negative factors regarding the acceptability to parents of lifelong education principles. Such studies point up areas where resistance might be felt or support relied on. They help to identify attitudes and beliefs that need to be changed.

Inferences Based on the Study of Learners

The final group of studies used learners as the data source. Two different approaches are possible in this case. First, one can simply ask students to report on their experiences in school, or even to evaluate from their personal perspective various aspects of the school according to the lifelong education criteria. On the other hand, one can try to derive inferences about the curriculum by assessing various characteristics of the learners, such as their attitudes toward learning or their special skills and competencies. This latter kind of study has the advantage of assessing actual outcomes at the level of the learner. Still, caution is appropriate when drawing inferences about the effects of school curriculum solely on the basis of learner characteristics, since factors other than the school can be influential as well. Both types of studies are contained in the national reports.

Reports by Learners on School Factors

Two of the national teams reported studies in which students described and evaluated aspects of their schooling.

Romania

The Romanian team conducted questionnaire and interview research on learners at the lower and upper secondary level. At the lower level data were collected from students at the 5th and 7th grade in the regular sample. The emphasis in this particular study was on aspects of the school programme the students found difficult, on extramural activity, and on signs of integration between learning in and out of the classroom. Topical headings for various sub-sections of the questionnaire included: "How I get along with my peers", "How I behave in learning", "How I am graded", "About my teachers", "About my parents", "What I do in my spare time", "What I read", "What I learn from", "How I take notes", "How I check my learning", "How I learn", "What I shall be able to do", and "How I take part in community activities".

Learners in the fifth grade reported, for example, that the fields of geography and history were most extensively sup-

plemented by out-of-class reading and by watching television.
There was also some relationship for the field of biology. The
7th grade students had a similar report for history and geography, but indicated that their most extensive utilization of
extramural resources involved exposure to foreign languages via
the medium of television. Data were also reported by students
on utilization of various types of museums and other community
resources, community service activities, and participation in
productive work activities.

At the upper secondary level the emphasis was somewhat
different. Data were collected on students in the 9th and 11th
years. Sections of the questionnaire included learning objectives of students, personal and social issues in which the student was interested, personal evaluation of various aspects of
the school programme, needed areas of personal development for
coping with the school programme, modes of study, assessment
of evaluation methods of teachers, evaluation of text-books,
and qualities appreciation in teachers.

Illustrative results include the fact that first year pupils at the upper level (9th grade) rated as their first school-
related priority the development of knowledge in specific subject areas, while students at the 11th grade level were more
concerned about being prepared for higher educational institutions. Students also desired (at both levels) opportunities to
discuss and participate in the solution of problems that con-
front adolescents such as the choice of a future profession
and learning how to use spare time. They were also interested
in learning more about young people in other countries. With
respect to the school, older students would like to have greater opportunity to talk with their teachers on matters relating
to intellectual learning. The most admired personal models
were teachers who exemplify character, followed by teachers
who help students think and act independently.

Overall, the Romanian report found older students oriented toward desirable role models and highly motivated toward
developing personal skills, includings those involving independent work and study.

The above are positive findings, although it is difficult in these and other national studies to establish what is
an ideal level for any of the factors assessed. An important
contribution for future research on evaluation for lifelong
education would be to establish a more quantitative basis for

structural concepts such as horizontal integration as well as for aspects of personal development. While it is certainly possible at present to find out that a given principle has not been implemented at all or has been implemented to only a trivial degree, it is not easy to establish that something exists to a sufficient or desirable degree. The ability to generate the latter type of conclusion would be extremely useful in any evaluation.

Sweden

Ljung, et al., (1973) used the direct procedure of asking students who had completed basic school four years earlier to answer a series of questions about what they had learned from the basic school curriculum. For each statement they indicated whether there had been more than enough, or not enough emphasis. In general, respondents indicated that there had been enough emphasis on straightforward knowledge goals. Goals rated as insufficiently emphasized were more general in nature and stressed social, interpersonal and economic knowledge. The Swedish report interpreted this response as evidence of support for lifelong educational goals among recent school graduates.

Studies of Characteristics of Learners

Both the Japanese and Swedish reports describe research studies undertaken in order to derive inferences about curriculum from empirically assessed characteristics of learners.

Japan

The Japanese team conducted an intensive study of learners, and this line of work has since been carried further by Kajita (1976). This is perhaps the most important single piece of research from the perspective of the Japanese team, because it deals with the concept of "personal growth", the key component of lifelong education in the conception of the Japanese researchers. The concept itself was stated in a way that incorporated motivation for improvement through self-initiated activities plus the skills and habits that are needed if such motivation is to be realized.

It was reported earlier that the Japanese team elaborated the abstract, verbal criterion statements by developing measures rather than by deriving more specific written criterion statements. This was illustrated in the 48 item questionnaire on personal growth and the accompanying shorter questionnaire on activities of a self-educative nature described in Chapter 4 in the section on *Analytical Empirical Procedures* (see p.43). The factor analysis of the longer instrument was also described in that section, and the four self-growth factors of *Confidence/ Self-Acceptance* (Factor 1), *Achievement Motivation* (Factor 2), *Dependence on External Judgment* (Factor 3), and *Desire and Efforts for Improvement* (Factor 4) were briefly illustrated (see p.45). These factors represent empirically based formulations of the personal growth concept stressed by the Japanese research team. Measures of the factors served as personal growth criteria in the study of learners to be described here.

Factor scores were computed for all respondents on each of the four personal growth factors. This procedure gave the relative standing of each learner with respect to each of the four aspects of personal growth. These scores were first used to make cross-sectional comparisons between the personal growth scores of learners, separately for boys and girls and across the various grade levels. To achieve this, average factor scores were calculated by school for each sex at each grade level. This made it possible to compare attitudes and feelings relating to personal growth in boys vs. girls, between schools in different regions, and between different grade levels.

Without doubt the most surprising finding of this particular analysis was that the average scores of all groups on the first or *Confidence/Self-Acceptance* factor went down as the grade level went up. That is, pupils in lower and upper secondary grades described themselves as less self-confident and accepting than did pupils in the elementary level (5th grade). *Achievement Motivation* (Factor 2) does not differ between grade levels for schools in the Tokyo area, but tended to decrease for higher levels in the provincial schools. Girls tended to score higher than boys at all levels in *Desire and Efforts for Improvement* (Factor 4), although less so at higher grade levels. Scores on this factor also decrease at higher levels of schooling. This decrease in efforts for improvement with grade level was confirmed in additional analyses which grouped individual students in terms of their joint pattern of scores on this and the achievement motivation factors, e.g. high on achievement motivation but low on desire for improvement, etc.

On the one hand, these results could be interpreted as indicating that secondary school students are more realistic about their own potential than are younger students and that the decline in average scores for efforts for improvement reflects such increasing realism. This interpretation is advanced in the Japanese report. However, it is also noted that one of the basic goals of schooling, to increase motivation on the part of the students to grow and improve, may not be facilitated for many students.

In a similar vein, the Japanese team reported, from an analysis combining the two factors of *Confidence/Self-Acceptance* (Factor 1) and *Dependence on External Judgment* (Factor 3), that the number of people who are low in self-confidence and dependent on external judgment increases in secondary school. While this could also in part be interpreted as revealing the development of a more realistic view of self and the world, it is equally true that this kind of outcome does not represent the kind of "growth" that leads to self-directed or independent learning. This was noted in the Japanese report. In the analysis of the items on self-educative habits the Japanese team were generally interested in the kinds and frequencies of such activities and in their relation to levels and location of schooling. Here it is not surprising that there were often differences between Tokyo and provincial learners, with the former showing sharp increases in aspirations to attend college at the secondary level and the latter showing a reverse trend. Differences also existed in reading habits, use of private tutors, etc.

This analysis produced a variety of findings, but the one singled out as of most concern by the Japanese team related to the kind of life learners indicate they would prefer in the future. There was relatively high endorsement at both secondary school levels of the item reading "A person who always (tries) to improve his own abilities and solve his own personal problems". While this response was encouraging, it was to some extent counterbalanced by increased endorsement at the upper secondary school level of items describing life styles involving minimal effort, living at one's own pace, and a high degree of self-indulgence in personal life. The report concludes that these kinds of preference were a cause for concern.

In the conclusion to the studies of learner characteristics the Japanese report noted the need for further research into whether the diminution in self-confidence and desire for self-improvement noted in secondary school students merely reflected a temporarily strict attitude toward the self at a certain stage of growth. The report concluded that the nature of schooling would have to be carefully reconsidered if the results of later studies revealed an equally bleak picture in later stages of education or in young adulthood.

The other finding of major concern was the tendency for self-educative activities to be manifested mainly in students who planned to go on to college. The level of such activity in schools where most learners did not plan to go on to college and, by inference, in technical, industrial, and commercial secondary schools, was seen as generally unsatisfactory. More effective approaches to the development of achievement motivation, internal evaluative criteria, and habits of self-education appeared to be necessary.

Sweden

The Swedish team conducted a study of learners which produced findings that in part related closely to the Japanese work just discussed. Jernryd (1974) reported on a five year study of 5th, 7th and 9th grade students in the Swedish comprehensive schools. The study was designed to assess in students the ability to evaluate information critically, independence in thought and action, resistance to authoritarian attitudes and self-reliance. The Swedish report noted that these objectives corresponded closely to the Swedish team's MSR (maturity, self-realization) criterion category.

One aspect of the Swedish study focussed on perception of self as measured by discrepancies between "actual" and "ideal" ratings of self. Jernryd found that these discrepancies increased markedly in the 10 to 16 age range. It does not seem unreasonable to suggest that discrepancies between the perceived and the idealized self reflect in part self-confidence or self-acceptance. In this sense the Jernryd finding seems related to the Japanese observation that self-ratings on the *Confidence/Self-Acceptance* factor decreased at higher grade levels. Closer analysis in the Swedish study showed that the greater discrepancies between actual and ideal self could be explained by the fact that learners in higher grades had higher ideals than learners in lower grades. This was interpreted as reflecting increased awareness of self-potential leading to the setting of higher personal goals. The two national studies used different measures and methods of analysis and can therefore be compared only with caution. But it might turn out that the use of ratings of ideal vs. actual self could shed further light on the Japanese findings.

The Swedish study did not give an encouraging picture of

the development of the ability to evaluate information critically. In spite of the fact that there was much greater emphasis
in the curriculum at grade 7 and 9 on the development of such
abilities, learners at this level did not differ from learners
at grade 5. The report generally concluded that the fault probably did not lie with teachers who were following the Lgr 699
curriculum in this area, but with the curriculum itself. Cross
grade comparisons were also mainly negative in so far as they
revealed any trends in the development of independence in learners. On the other hand there was evidence that authoritarian,
rigid, and dogmatic attitudes as measured by psychological tests
declined as students grew older. Increasingly tolerant and re-
flective attitudes replaced moralizing or punishing attitudes
and dependence on authority for structure.

A major contribution of Jernryd's long term study lay in
the area of definitions of concepts and their measures. A variety of the latter were used, including bibliographical and attitudinal questionnaires, personality tests, teacher reports, and
situational tests in which the resistance of learners to suggestions and group pressure was revealed. In particular, the
components of the concept of independent learning behaviour
were explored. A concrete list of suggestions about components
of the curriculum likely to contribute to the independence of
learners was also provided at the end of the report.

Conclusion

This survey of the curriculum evaluation studies conducted or reviewed by the national teams has attempted to summarize
the main points of similarity and contrast in purpose and method as well as to give illustrative findings at the national
level. The lengthy and detailed English language national reports on which it is based were in the case of Japan and Romania briefer versions of the original national language reports.
As a result it has been impossible because of limitations in
space to cite all of the material in the national reports. However, the studies described here include the most important
work in the reports and give, we hope, a comprehensive picture
of the wide variety of approaches that can be applied in the
evaluation of curricula under the principles of lifelong education. Moreover, the procedures that have been described are by
no means limited to the evaluation of national curricula. They
can be applied at the regional or local level as well as in
countries with decentralized educational authorities.

The structure for classifying empirical evaluation studies developed at the beginning of the chapter appears to be a useful tool for summarizing diverse approaches to the evaluation of curricula. We began with the *formal or written curriculum* and saw that it was possible to evaluate it either by systematically classifying its elements of content into criterion categories or by asking various groups to interpret its intentions in terms of concrete implications for the classroom. The next class of studies looked at the operational curriculum from the point of view of the *actual practices and policies of schools.* Here the evaluation studies could be separated into those dealing with teaching vs. those dealing with other practices or policies. The third class of studies addressed the most complex curriculum of all, the *informal curriculum of family and community.* National studies in this category focussed entirely on parents, either by asking about what schools ought to accomplish or about what parents themselves try to accomplish in guiding the learning of their children. Finally, a fourth approach involved the *study of learners themselves* by obtaining descriptions of schools from learners or, alternatively, assessing the learners' abilities, attitudes and proclivities.

All of the possibilities are not exhausted by the above categories and sub-categories, but a surprising amount of ground has been covered. Most important, there is no need for curriculum evaluation studies to be entirely contained within a given category. The most powerful types of studies would combine categories, as for example when measures or school practices and policies are related to the characteristics of learners, as done in at least one of the studies described. Future research in this area should attempt to make these kinds of combination in the interests of arriving at statements of causal relationships.

NOTES

1. All titles of tables are quoted from the Swedish report.

2. See Note 1. in Chapter 4 for a brief statement about the purpose of factor analysis (p.61).

3. Factor scores in this case indicate the relative extent to which teachers at each school say they use each of the four evaluation or planning practices.

102   Curriculum Evaluation for Lifelong Education

REFERENCES

Averch, H.A.; Carroll, S.J.; Donaldson, T.S.; Kiesling,
H.J., and Pincus, J., *How Effective is Schooling? A
Critical Review and Synthesis of Research Findings.*
Santa Monica, Calif.: Rand Corp., 1972.

Axelsson, R., and Ekman, B., *Account of a National
Questionnaire. Part II.* Report from Educational De-
velopment Block, Uppsala, Sweden, No.4, 1973.
(In Swedish).

Bredhänge, G.; Gustafsson, B.; Hallin, G.; Ingvarson,
A.; Odhagen, T., and Stigebrandt, E., *Analysis of
the Didactic Process: Presentation of Aims, Design,
Experimental Groups and Measuring Instruments, together with some Descriptive Data.* Gothenburg: University, Department of Educational Research. Report
No.24, 1971. (In Swedish).

Bredhänge, G., and Odhagen, T., *Analysis of the Didactic
Process: A Study of Teacher and Student Behaviours in
the Classroom Situation.* Gothenburg: University,
Department of Educational Research. Report No.28,
1972. (In Swedish).

Eriksson, A. "Classroom Observations Focussed on Teaching Behaviours that Potentially Encourage Creativity:
Methods and Relation Studies in Grades 4-6." *Pedagogisk-Psykologiska Problems.* Malmö: School of Education,
University of Malmö, No.206, 1974. (In Swedish).

Jernryd, E. "Optimal Resistance to Authority and Propa-
ganda: A Study of Age and Sex Differences". *Pedagogisk-Psykologiska Problems.* Malmö: School of Education, University of Malmö, No.239, 1974. (In Swedish.
Briefer English version in *Didakometry and Sociometry,*
5, No.2, 1973, pp.28-53).

Kajita, E. "Development of Self-Growth Attitudes and
Habits in School Children". *Research Bulletin of the
National Institute for Educational Research.* Tokyo:
No.14, 1976, pp.27-43.

Ljung, B.O.; Lundman, L., and Emanuelsson, I., *Individual
- Society - Education.* Stockholm: Department of Educational Research, School of Education, 1973. (In Swedish).

Rosenshine, B., and Furst, N. "Research on Teacher Performance Criteria". In Smith, B.O. (ed.), *Research in Teacher Education: A Symposium*. Englewood Cliffs, N.J.: Prentice-Hall, 1971.

Stencrantz, A.; Svingby, G., and Wallin, E. *What Do we Want of the School? - Background to and Interpretation of the Overall Goals of the School*. Gothenburg: Department of Educational Research, Gothenburg University. Report No.87, 1973. (In Swedish).

CHAPTER 6

STEPS TOWARD THE PREPARATION OF PLANS FOR IMPROVING NATIONAL CURRICULA

In Chapter 3 the function of evaluation was described as one of facilitating decision-making and policy formulation. Decisions are thought of here as specific, concrete, and situation-bound. Policies, in turn, are seen as principles which guide or mediate potentially large numbers of decisions. When the phenomena being evaluated are very large in scope, as are national curricula, it is more realistic to think in terms of contributions to the formulation of policy rather than to highly concrete decision-making. The final sections of the three national reports reflect this fact.

Each of the national evaluation studies operated with the support and approval of central authority. Two were conducted at national research institutes and the third, though based in a university research laboratory, was carried out with the support of a national education board. In each country the studies were defined as pilot efforts, experiments in the development and application of lifelong education criteria. Their purpose was not that of preparing actual plans for reform, but rather to develop criteria and procedures for determining what kinds of reform would be required in an educational system organized according the principles of lifelong education.

The conclusions to the three national reports took somewhat different forms. The Japanese emphasized the further development of the evaluation criteria and the design of full scale evaluation studies. The Romanians projected the basic organizational forms that would be useful in implementing any proposed reforms. The Swedes stressed the role of adult education as well as the type of basic research that would be needed in order to develop further individual propensities toward lifelong learning. (It will be recalled that the Swedish report used the concept of "lifelong learning" rather than "lifelong education".) The conclusions will be summarized separately.

Japan: For the Development of Evaluation Capabilities

The Japanese team assigned the participation of each of its individual members to one of the four areas studied: written curriculum, latent curriculum (mainly based on data contributed by teachers), parents' attitudes and aspirations, and personal growth in learners. To some degree individuals working in each area arrived at their own interpretations of the evaluation criteria. In the time available it was not possible for the team as a whole fully to agree on a common set of interpretations. This was seen as a first priority for later work at the National Institute.

A two level approach, one theoretical, the other empirical, was proposed for the further development of the criteria. The former would continue the analysis of lifelong education as a concept until a set of educational assumptions and principles fully acceptable to all participants could be derived. The empirical approach to the development of criteria would continue along the path taken in the first Japanese report, describing and interpreting actual practices in schools, homes and communities in the search for more concrete kinds of criteria. Ultimately, the theoretical and empirical would be combined into a single criterion list.

In addition, research designs for evaluating the curriculum in the context of real learning situations would be developed on the basis of experience gained in the first Japanese study. Considerable emphasis was placed on the need to evaluate the operational curriculum in all its manifestations. In this sense, the proposals for future work formulated by the Japanese team are direct extensions of the initial study.

Romania: Structures for Implementation

The Romanian report in its conclusions reflected a national context in which curriculum reform is anticipated. Romania is presently in the process of extending the period of compulsory schooling from 8 to 10 years (to 12 years by 1990) as well as increasing the kindergarten network. The report views reform as an evolutionary process growing out of existing structures. Adult education was seen as the institutional structure with potential for making the greatest contribution. Adult education in Romania is presently divided into vocational training, evening school and extra-mural studies and general cultural educational activities organized regionally and through trade unions. The conclusions to the report particularly emphasize the potential relevance to the schools of experience gained in professional training centres operating during the last four years in fields such as engineering, medical services, engineering (agricultural) and management. This again reflects the broader emphasis in the report on links between the school curriculum and production and research.

Responsibility for the development and maintenance of a strategy of improvement and innovation is assigned by the Romanian report to a special commission within the Ministry of Education and Instruction and along lines established earlier in 1971 with legislation on the improvement of vocational training. This body would set priorities for innovation and define stages of change, monitor resources and financing, inform decision-making bodies, etc.

Finally, the report proposes 6 vehicles for shaping the school curriculum in accordance with principles of lifelong education:

1) *Publications* of a professional type describing innovations in theory and method as well as mass-distribution publications particularly emphasizing the contributions of teaching staff

2) *Experimental schools* emphasizing research, development and demonstration

3) *Teacher training* at all levels (primary, secondary and adult) under a common curriculum stressing the role of the teacher as a manager of an educational environment as well as a model for continuing self-improvement, plus emphasis at the secondary level on integrated or interdisciplinary approaches to knowledge, relationships with work and production and the development of skills in the application of educational technology

4) *Dissemination* through conferences, pamphlets and revised school documents distributed to teachers and principals

5) *Symposia*, involving scientists and educators and aimed at the generation of ideas for research and development, and

6) *Legislation* relating to teacher training and teaching practice.

The Romanian report concludes with a suggested timetable for distributing the above activities up to the year 1990.

Sweden: Recurrent Education and Research on Autonomous Learning

The Swedish report concluded that the written curriculum was generally favourable to the application of lifelong education principles, but that the everyday life of the school by no means presented such a sanguine picture. Implementation at the level of the school was seen as a central problem, though one whose solution in itself would still not assure the maintenance of lifelong learning on a societal scale. The latter is dependent on how people behave after leaving school and here institutions and structures responsible for recurrent education have a large role to play. The Swedish report parallels that of Romania in that adult education was viewed as bearing a heavy responsibility for providing many of the means for lifelong learning to the school population.

Reviewing the existing resources for recurrent education, the Swedish report noted that a variety of opportunities already existed in municipal adult education, training for the labour market, internal training in industry and universities, and to a considerable extent in the armed forces where training is in principle organized on a recurrent basis. The People's High Schools (or "Folkhögskolor") and the adult education associations were cited as representing institutional forms of adult education which are most compatible with the principles of lifelong education. The need for revisions in curriculum and organization of other forms was also implied in the report.

Finally, the Swedish report called for research into patterns of independent learning that occur outside of formal organizations like the school, both for individuals and groups. The authors suggest that relatively little is known about the personal characteristics and mode of operation of independent learners, yet presumably these are precisely the kinds of individuals that lifelong education seeks to produce. This seems to be a potentially fruitful suggestion. A start has been made in the work of Tough (1975) and others on adult learners and the kinds of project they engage in. Certainly much more information is needed on their characteristics and their background as well as a closely associated, but equally vast, domain of inquiry into the relationship between environmental factors and autonomy in learning.

REFERENCE

Tough, A., *The Adult's Learning Projects*. Toronto: The Ontario Institute for Studies in Education, 1971. Research in Education Series No.1.

CHAPTER 7

CONCLUSION

A useful way to end this report is to consider the question of what has been accomplished in the project as a whole. In this regard it is especially relevant to recall from Chapter 1 that only a few years ago Lengrand (1970) expressed grave concern that the then excessively theoretical nature of the dialogue about lifelong education could generate scepticism about the concept and ultimately block the emergence of widespread support for its implementation. This author saw an urgent need for the exploration of concrete "situations, structures, (and) problems".

It is fair to say that the three national studies on which this report is based easily represent the longest stride that has yet been taken in the direction of concretizing the meaning of lifelong education. The studies are of course in part an application of earlier analytical work on what have been referred to here and elsewhere as the "concept characteristics" of lifelong education, but they also extend and elaborate on that work through the medium of empirical evaluation research. It has been pointed out at a number of points that the reports by the national teams are modest in their conclusions. Criteria lists are seen as requiring further development; instruments and procedures are described as preliminary, and most findings are reported tentatively. None of these qualifications detracts from the fact that the reports in their collectivity break new ground.

More than anything else, the national studies address the fundamental question of whether or not it is possible to distinguish between events and conditions that are characteristic of lifelong education and those which are not. The "vagueness, formlessness and imprecision" referred to by Lengrand (1970) has not been entirely dispelled perhaps, but certainly the line of work of which these studies are the most recent

109

representatives has helped considerably to demonstrate that the concept can be applied to the evaluation of various aspects of school curricula in the significant sense of defining what is to be measured and how the resulting findings are to be interpreted. Evaluation is in many ways the most critical test of any educational concept or set of principles. If the latter are not clear enough to lead to distinctions between what is, or is not, desirable, then they are also useless as guides to praxis.

Another kind of scepticism also arises, however. Granted that all three teams managed to develop and apply criteria that successfully distinguished between the desirable and undesirable, it still may be that the resulting distinctions were not unique. In other words, had the members of the national teams never heard of the principles of lifelong education, would they have used essentially the same criteria, proceeded in the same fashion, and arrived at conclusions that did not differ in substance from the conclusions of the present reports?

Again, the answer appears to be reasonably favourable, though with at least one important qualification. It has to be recognized that lifelong education is not an entirely new concept. As a matter of fact, it incorporates a great many educational principles that have been advanced in the recent past and that have in many cases been, at least in part, operationalized. The uniqueness of the lifelong education principles lies not in their individual originality, but rather in their inclusiveness and relative emphasis. Lifelong education is really an amalgam of a great variety of ideas about education put together in a way that hopefully anticipates developments in various types of societies. It is *new* in the sense of its comprehensiveness, inclusiveness and emphasis rather than in terms of its individual elements. In this situation it is inevitable that many of the individual criteria utilized by the national teams would appear on similar lists generated by contemporary educators who were not necessarily operating within the framework of lifelong education. So, many of the specific evaluative criteria and resulting findings cannot possibly be unique to curriculum evaluation under lifelong education.

Still, it is unlikely that most evaluations, even of something as broad as the national curriculum, would develop lists of criteria as comprehensive as those used in the national studies, if without the lifelong education framework. There is also the matter of emphasis. Certainly the various kinds of horizontal and vertical linkages in structure and organization

implied in the *Horizontal Integration* and *Vertical Articulation*
clusters would not be so strongly emphasized in evaluations proceeding from less comprehensive conceptual bases. Likewise,
there is probably much more emphasis in the present studies on
the development of generalized or open-ended personal growth
characteristics in learners rather than on measuring the accumu-
lation of concrete knowledge. As a matter of fact, it is significant that none of the three national studies utilized any traditional types of achievement measures. While this might be dis-
pleasing to many traditionalists in education, it is an under-
standable and predictable result of developing evaluative criteria under the lifelong education perspective.

It is also evident that much more emphasis was given in
the national evaluations to testing the climate for changes
than would be the case for evaluative efforts operating under
different principles. Ordinarily evaluations would be more concerned with assessing the extent to which existing educational
goals and objectives were being realized. This was true in the
present studies where existing goals abstracted from the national curricula were consistent with one or more of the lifelong education criteria. But in addition, there were a variety
of efforts to assess the openness of teachers, parents, and
learners to lifelong educational principles that have not yet
been legitimatized in the popular conception of the role of the
school. Again, the emphasis given to the assessment of the climate for particular types of change is reasonably unique in the
studies summarized here. It is fair to conclude, then, that
there are important qualitative differences in the scope, emphasis, and findings of the three national curriculum evaluations that can be attributed directly to the fact that they
were conducted within the framework of lifelong education.

Finally, the national studies taken together have been
successful in demonstrating that there are a variety of sources
that can be utilized in evaluating existing curricula according
to lifelong education criteria. The breakdown in Chapter 5 of
empirical evaluation studies into the four categories of studies of the written curriculum, studies of the practices and
policies of schools, studies of the informal curriculum of family and community, and studies of the learners themselves reveals just how comprehensive the national evaluations really
were in their combined version. Likewise, the variety of instruments and procedures utilized in the studies provides a
rich illustration for others who may follow similar work in
their respective countries or localities.

The value of multinational research and development efforts that operate from similar frameworks and with common goals but allow for diversity of approach is readily apparent. The authors of this report have been able to explore and compare a wide range of approaches to evaluate national curricula under the framework of lifelong education as a result of the different perspectives that entered into the national efforts. Most important, however, is the fact that the national studies were designed as evaluations. Evaluation demands specificity and as a result the national studies constitute genuinely meaningful steps in the direction of concretizing the principles of lifelong education.

APPENDICES

APPENDICES

APPENDIX 1

NATIONAL RESEARCH TEAMS AND REPORTS

The English language versions of the three national curriculum evaluation reports are cited below along with the names of the researchers who produced them. The English language reports themselves were in all three cases printed in limited quantities.

JAPAN: *Development of Criteria and Procedures for Evaluation of School Curricula in the Perspective of Lifelong Education.* Tokyo: National Institute for Educational Research, 1975.

Research Staff

Yoshihiko Arimoto
Ikuo Arai
Masashi Fujita
Kazuo Ishizaka
Eiichi Kajita
Koji Kato
Kentaro Kihara (Co-Director)
Joji Kikuchi
Shigeo Masui (Co-Director)
Koichi Miyazaki
Tadanobu Yamaguchi

ROMANIA: *Development of Criteria and Procedures for Evaluation of School Curricula in the Perspective of Lifelong Education.* Bucharest: Institute of Pedagogical and Psychological Research, 1975.

Research Staff

Gheorghe Bunescu
Alexandru Darie
Ana-Maria Ichim
Pavel Muresan
Costache Olareanu (Research Officer)
Victoria Popovici
Camelia Rosculet

116   Curriculum Evaluation for Lifelong Education

Leon Topa (Research Officer)
Ion Verdes

SWEDEN: *Lifelong Learning in Swedish Curricula.*
Malmö, Sweden: School of Education, Department of Educational and Psychological Research, 1975. (Didakometry, No.48).
(English version and direct translation of Fredriksson, L. and Gestrelius, K. "Det livslanga lärandet i de svenska läroplanerna". *Pedagogisk-psykologiska Problems.* Malmö: Lärarhögskolan, Nr.274, 1975.)

Research Staff and Authors

Lennart Fredriksson
Kurt Gestrelius

APPENDIX 2

A LIST OF CONCEPT CHARACTERISTICS OF LIFELONG EDUCATION

1. The three basic terms upon which the *meaning* of the concept is based are *life, lifelong* and *education*. The meaning attached to these terms and the interpretation given to them largely determine the scope and meaning of lifelong education. (*Meaning* and *Operational Modality*).

2. Education does not terminate at the end of formal schooling but it is a *lifelong process*. Lifelong education covers the entire life-span of an individual.

3. Lifelong education is not confined to adult education but it encompasses and unifies all stages of education - pre-primary, primary, secondary and so forth, thus it seeks to view *education* in its *totality*.

4. Lifelong education includes *formal, non-formal* and *informal patterns of education*.

5. The *home* plays the first, most subtle and crucial role in initiating the process of lifelong learning. This continues throughout the entire life-span of an individual through a process of *family learning*.

6. The *community* also plays an important role in the system of lifelong education right from the time the child begins to interact with it, and continues its education function both in professional and general areas throughout life.

7. The *institutions of education* like schools, universities and training centres are of course important, but only as one of the agencies for lifelong education. They no longer enjoy the monopoly of educating the people and can no longer exist in isolation from other educative agencies in the society.

8. Lifelong education seeks continuity and articulation along its vertical or longitudinal dimension. (*Vertical Articulation*).

9. Lifelong education also seeks integration at its horizontal

117

and depth dimensions at every stage in life. (*Horizontal Integration*).

10. Contrary to the elitist form of education, lifelong education is *universal* in character. It represents *democratization of education*.

11. Lifelong education is characterized by its *flexibility* and *diversity* in *content, learning tools* and *techniques,* and *time* of learning.

12. Lifelong education is a *dynamic approach* to education which allows adaptation of materials and media of learning as and when new developments take place.

13. Lifelong education allows *alternative patterns* and forms of acquiring education.

14. Lifelong education has two broad components: *general* and *professional*. These components are not completely different from each other but are *inter-related* and *interactive* in nature.

15. The *adaptive* and *innovative functions* of the individual and the society are fulfilled through lifelong education.

16. Lifelong education carries out a *corrective function*: to take care of the shortcomings of the existing system of education.

17. The ultimate goal of lifelong education is to maintain and improve the *quality of life*.

18. There are three major *prerequisites* for lifelong education, namely, *opportunity, motivation* and *educability*.

19. Lifelong education is an *organizing principle* for all education.

20. At the *operational level*, lifelong education provides a *total* system of *all* education.

+   Quoted from Dave, R.H., *Lifelong Education and School Curriculum*. Hamburg: Unesco Institute for Education, 1973. (uie monographs 1).

APPENDIX 3

CURRICULUM COMPONENTS FOR THE EVALUATION OF SCHOOL CURRICULA IN THE PERSPECTIVE OF LIFELONG EDUCATION

First International Workshop
Hamburg: 18-28 February 1974

In order to evolve an operational procedure for curriculum evaluation, it is necessary to identify major curriculum components around which criteria, procedures and instruments of evaluation can be developed. There is no one way of categorizing the total field of curriculum into different components. The curriculum components suggested below, therefore, provide only a starting point for discussion.

The curriculum components have been further divided into sub-components for delineating and delimiting the scope of each component and also for capturing different aspects of the total curriculum.

1. OBJECTIVES

   A) Statement of Objectives

      1.1 Overall objectives
      1.2 Objectives for entire school stage
      1.3 Stage-wise objectives (primary, secondary, etc.)
      1.4 Subject-wise objectives

   B) Formulation of Objectives

      Procedures of formulating different statements of objectives at the national, sub-national and local (school) level.

2. CURRICULUM PLAN

   A) Statement of Curriculum Plan (Syllabus/Courses of Study)

      2.1 Curriculum design (rationale, curriculum areas, diversification, internal differentiation, time allocation, etc.)
      2.2 Curriculum contents for individual curri-

119

culum areas (selection and organization
of content, integration with other subjects).

2.3 Other aspects, if any, included in the
curriculum plan.

B) Curriculum Planning Process

Procedures of curriculum planning adopted at
the national, sub-national and school levels
for various sub-stages and subjects.

3. TEACHING AND LEARNING ACTIVITIES

3.1 Classroom activities (individual, group,
pupil-centred, teacher directed, etc.)
3.2 Activities between classes of the same
grade (where applicable)
3.3 Inter-grade activities
3.4 School level activities
3.5 Inter-school activities
3.6 Activities with community
3.7 Activities with family
3.8 Activities with educational users.

4. LEARNING MATERIALS

4.1 Text-books (content selection, design,
sequencing, presentation, illustrations,
exercises, format, etc.)
4.2 Other learning aids in the school (including audio-visual aids, laboratories,
school library, etc.)
4.3 Use of out-of-school learning resources.

5. EVALUATION PROCEDURES

5.1 Evaluation during the school year (internal,
formal, informal, continuous, teacher-made,
standardized, etc.)
5.2 Evaluation at end of the school year (where
applicable, for promotion to the next grade)
5.3 Evaluation at the end of a school stage
(where applicable) through external agencies
5.4 Other aspects and procedures of evaluation.

6. CURRICULUM IMPLEMENTATION

6.1 Planning and preparation for implementation at the national and sub-national levels (diffusion, phasing, time and other resources, techniques and staff)

6.2 Planning and preparation for implementation at the school level (re-organization of school programme, replenishing equipment, etc.)

6.3 Teacher preparation (involvement re-orientation, self study, availability of new curricula and materials)

6.4 Involvement of school supervisors, other administrators, professional organizations, parents, community, etc.

6.5 Periodical evaluation and strengthening of the implementation programme.

APPENDIX 4

EVALUATIVE CRITERIA FOR CURRICULUM COMPONENTS

First International Workshop
Hamburg: 18-28 February 1974

1. OBJECTIVES (Revised)

Evaluative Criteria	Explanation
1. Co-ordination with the home	Complementary roles of the home and the school.
	Unique role and responsibility of the school in the context of the home
	Preparation for future parental role.
	Parental involvement in daily programme of the school.
	Parental involvement in the development of the school programme.
	Recognition of the need to provide mechanisms to co-ordinate home with school.
2. Co-ordination with the local community	Contribution of the school to the solution of community problems (moral and social) and vice versa.
	Study of community problems (including study of community conditions).
	Use of community resources and facilities in educational programme.
	Community activities in the school.

Evaluative Criteria

Explanation

Use of school facilities and resources by community,

Preparation for community role (for adult life more generally).

Development of relationship with out-of-school youth organizations, social welfare committees, etc.

Encouragement of tolerance and fostering of value orientation suited to productive participation in community life.

3. Co-ordination with the larger society

The term larger society includes the regional, national and international community.

Study of the national, sub-national and international problems.

Study of strategies for confronting national, sub-national and international problems.

Study of how problems are attacked by various institutions, agencies and individuals.

Study of ways and means by which individuals at different age-levels can participate in solving social problems.

Preparation for role as citizen.

4. Co-ordination with the world of work

Attitude towards work, production, etc.

Work for monetary returns, work for social and personal returns.

Early awareness of the world of work bringing monetary and non-monetary returns.

Evaluative Criteria	Explanation
	Direct and broad-based experience with the world of work.
5. Articulation with the pre-school experience	Readiness to profit from school experience.
	Provision for remedial devices where needed.
6. Articulation with the post-school learning	Adequate preparation for immediate and lifelong learning.
	Linkage with higher learning.
	Availability of guidance services.
7. Articulation with the parallel forms of learning	Consideration of organized learning opportunities available outside the school as parallel programmes.
	Lateral transfer and multi-entry system.
8. Enhancement of educability	Developing competence in adopting varied learning strategies such as self-learning, inter-learning, etc.
	Development of basic learning skills like observation, purposeful reading, etc.
	Development of basic intellectual and psychomotor skills such as critical thinking, interpretation, muscular co-ordination for manual activities, etc.
	Use of a variety of media, materials and aids with ease and discrimination.
	Identification of learning needs and competence in planning, conducting and evaluating one's own study.

Evaluative Criteria	Explanation
	Fostering positive attitude towards self-growth and community growth.
	Development of knowledge of oneself, one's limitations, self-insights, etc. for self improvement.
9. Enhancement of interest in learning	Attitude of inquiry and inquisitiveness.
	Responding favourably to new learning needs and programmes.
	Taking initiative and active participation in learning activities.
	Encouraging others to get involved in a learning activity.
	Awakening of interests among others in one's social environment.
10. Promotion of flexibility	Provision for local adaptation of objectives.
	Encouragement of openness among students.
	Provision for alternative approaches in curriculum planning and implementation.
	Provision of alternative forms and structures of educational services.
	Encouragement of participation of students and teachers in educational decision-making.
11. Exposure to broad areas of learning	Initiation into a variety of fields of study.
	Understanding the inter-disciplinary relationship among different subjects.

Evaluative Criteria	Explanation
	Developing competence in adopting the tools of learning and methods of inquiry in different subjects.
12. Individualization of learning	Recognition of individual differences in learning.
	Provision of different learning and evaluating strategies to accommodate different learning styles.
13. Emphasis on multi-dimensional, balanced growth of individuals	Development of emotional, social, aesthetic, physical and manual abilities.
	Enhancement of adaptive functions and coping skills.
14. Understanding and renewal of value system	Promotion of future orientedness, open-mindedness and models of self-growth, etc.
	Emphasis on self examination of one's own value system, and that of one's community.
	Adoption of a progressive, self-renewing value system.
15. Promotion of creativity and innovativeness	Development of an attitude of experimentation.
	Promotion of divergent thinking styles.
	Development of ability to generate and direct change.

APPENDIX 5

FORM FOR COMBINING CURRICULUM COMPONENTS AND EVALUATIVE CRITERIA

Components / Evaluative Criteria	Objectives	Curriculum Plan	Teaching Methods and Learning Activities	Evaluation & Guidance	Curriculum Implementation
1. Horizontal Integration - home - world of work - community - larger society - mass media - among subjects of study - among aspects of development such as physical, moral, intellectual, etc.					
2. Vertical Articulation - with post-school experience for adult education - with pre-school experience - between different levels of school - within a subject among different grades - within individual aspects of development (physical, intellectual, etc.) along the time dimension					
3. Individual and Collective Growth - self reconstruction - understanding and renewal of value system - multi-dimensional growth (biological, social, moral, vocational, etc.)					
4. Autodidactic (Self-directed Learning) - self-learning - inter-learning - guided learning - educability or readiness for further learning					
5. Other Aspects - creativity, innovativeness - flexibility - diversity - provision for alternatives					

127

APPENDIX 6

COMBINED LIST OF CRITERIA AND ILLUSTRATIVE SPECIFICATIONS

I. Horizontal Integration

Functional integration of all social agencies having educational roles not only among elements of the curriculum at any given level but also among learners with different personal characteristics:

Criterion 1. Integration between school and home

Specifications:

1. School and home maintain complementary roles in education of the child.

2. School and home work co-operatively to improve the quality of education.

Criterion 2. Integration between school and community

Specifications:

1. Curriculum is related to social and developmental problems.

2. School plays an appropriate role in helping to solve community problems.

3. Community facilities, resources and experience are used for school activities.

Criterion 3. Integration between school and world of work

Specifications:

1. School helps to develop positive attitudes in learners toward participation in work and production.

2. School activities are related to actual production through study visits and trainee periods at different places of work.

3. Learners are given information and advice concerning their future studies and careers.

Criterion 4. Integration between school and cultural institutions, organizations and activities

Specifications:

1. Interests and skills of learners are developed for an active cultural life.

2. Learners make a contribution to the cultural life of their community.

3. Films, theatre, music, museums, libraries and sport are incorporated in the school curriculum.

Criterion 5. Integration between school and mass media

Specifications:

1. Full use is made of mass media as teaching device in school activities.

2. Ability is developed in learners to evaluate critically information presented via mass media.

Criterion 6. Integration of subjects of study

Specifications:

1. Humanistic and scientific cultures are correlated within the curriculum.

2. Different school subjects are integrated into wider fields of study.

3. Redundancy in subjects is eliminated.

4. Learners are enabled to understand the relation between different parts of the curriculum.

Criterion 7. Integration between curricular subjects and extra-curricular activities

Specifications:

1. Integration between intra- and extra-curricular activities and the interests which learners develop in their future careers is maintained.

2. Learners' interest in the use of leisure is maintained.

3. Learners acquire skills for use in leisure.

4. Learners develop ability to choose appropriate occupations in work or leisure.

Criterion 8. Integration of learners having different characteristics

Specifications:

1. Learners of different ethnic, physical, intellectual, religious and social characteristics jointly participate in the learning process.

2. Learners understand the need to reconcile different ethnic, physical, intellectual, religious and social characteristics in one society.

II. Vertical Integration

Articulation among curriculum components at different levels of schooling and between school curricula and pre- and post-school education:

Criterion 1. Integration between pre-school experiences and the school

Specifications:

1. Experiences of learners before and after entering school are linked.

2. Interest in future school learning is awakened with visits to school and other extra-curricular incentives.

Criterion 2. Integration between different grades or other levels within the school

Specifications:

1. Organization and study content at

different school levels are linked
systematically.

2. Curriculum content is organized to
ensure continuity, and smooth transfer at each level.

3. Curriculum is structured at lower
levels so as to allow all learners
a variety of options at higher levels.

3. School is organized as united basic
school instead of as a parallel
school system.

Criterion 3. <u>Integration between school and post-school
activities</u>

Specifications:

1. Learners concern themselves with
their future careers.

2. Learners are informed about organization, operation and entrance requirements of different forms of
adult education.

3. School gives learners practical experience of some main activities of
society in its programmes and organization.

4. Learners understand rapid tempo of
change in world for which they are
preparing themselves.

5. Curriculum is co-ordinated with different forms of adult education to
ensure smooth transfer.

III. <u>Orientation of Self-Growth</u>

Development in learners of personal characteristics
that contribute to a long-term process of growth and development including realistic self-awareness, interest in
the world and in other people, the desire to achieve, internalized criteria for making evaluation and judgments,
and overall integration of the personality:

Criterion 1. <u>Self-understanding</u>

Specifications:

1. Learners are aware of responsibility for own growth.

2. Learners explore new areas for their development and growth.

3. Learners acquire confidence from a better understanding of their capacities.

Criterion 2. <u>Interest in human beings and in environmental world</u>

Specifications:

1. Learners are interested in their physical and biological environment.

2. Learners are interested in the variety of human conditions.

3. Learners are interested in their community, nation and international environment.

Criterion 3. <u>Achievement motivation</u>

Specifications:

1. Learners are motivated to improve their own abilities (cognitive, affective and psychomotor).

2. Learners are motivated to attain certain concrete goals.

Criterion 4. <u>Establishment of internal judgment criteria</u>

Specifications:

1. Learners acquire standards by which to exercise judgment.

2. Learners are able to formulate opinions independently.

3. Learners develop a realistic appreciation of the value of their judgment in different areas.

Criterion 5. Establishment of progressive values
and attitudes

Specifications:

1. Learners establish future-oriented
values and attitudes.

2. Learners develop flexible thinking
and tolerance.

3. Learners are willing to consider
varying alternatives.

Criterion 6. Integration of personality

Specifications:

1. Learners explore and assimilate an
ideal model for personal development.

2. Learners seek to attain an all-round
personal maturity.

3. Learners seek to make their own contribution to the development of
human society.

IV. Self-Directed Learning

Individualization of the learning experience toward
the goal of developing the learner's own skills and competencies in the planning, execution and evaluation of learning activities both as an individual and as a member of a
cooperative learning group.

Criterion 1. Participation in the planning, execution and
evaluation of learning

Specifications:

1. Learners participate in planning of
learning on basis of needs of group
as well as of self.

2. Learners are involved in planning
both school and out-of-school activities.

3. Learners are involved in improving
execution of various learning activities.

4. Learners participate in planning evaluation of individual and group learning procedures.

Criterion 2. Individualization of learning

Specifications:

1. Differences between individuals in learning ability and learning styles are given consideration.

2. Maturity, previous knowledge, interest and other characteristics of learners are given consideration.

3. Organizational facilities are provided for making individualized teaching and learning practicable.

4. The content and materials of learning are so organized as to make individual learning possible.

Criterion 3. Development of self-learning skills

Specifications:

1. Enquiry learning is promoted.

2. Opportunity is provided for practising necessary techniques (e.g. observation, purposeful reading, note-taking, classification).

3. Opportunity is provided for use of a variety of learning sources, media and materials.

4. Opportunity is provided for learners to identify their own learning needs and to formulate learning objectives.

5. Opportunity is provided for learners to identify their own appropriate styles and procedures of learning.

Criterion 4. Development of inter-learning skills

Specifications:

1. Learners share responsibility in the

learning-teaching process.

2. Opportunity is provided for learners to work and play in teams.

3. Opportunity is provided for learners to participate in activities of groups which are heterogeneous (e.g. in age, knowledge, skill), and of different size.

Criterion 5. Development of self-evaluation and co-operative evaluation skills

Specifications:

1. Learners understand need for evaluation.

2. Learners accept self-evaluation as integral part of system of evaluation.

3. Learners accept evaluation by others as complement of self-evaluation.

4. Group or individual work is evaluated co-operatively.

5. Opportunity is provided for learners to obtain experience with different evaluation procedures and purposes.

V. Democratization

Equality of educational opportunity; opportunity to participate in decision-making and in the teaching/learning process despite differences in status; the humane exercise of authority, and the encouragement of creativity, divergent thinking, flexibility and curiosity on the part of the learners:

Criterion 1. Equality of educational opportunity for all regardless of personal differences

Specifications:

1. Opportunity is available equally regardless of sex, race, religion, social background and physical characteristics.

2. Special help is provided for those unable to take full advantage of this equality.

3. School fosters tolerance of personal differences.

Criterion 2. <u>Sharing of decision-making and other types of involvement in the teaching/learning process among participants with different status and roles *vis à vis* the school</u>

Specifications:

1. Parents, community, teachers and learners participate in school organization and administration.

2. School recognizes value of contributions by community members in teaching/learning process.

Criterion 3. <u>Humane exercise of authority</u>

Specifications:

1. Discipline results from consensus of staff and pupils.

2. Overloaded programmes are avoided.

3. Non-punitive evaluation functions and methods are stressed.

4. Learners evaluate teaching for its improvement.

5. Authority receives support from moral and civic education.

Criterion 4. <u>Encouragement of creativity and flexibility</u>

Specifications:

1. Curiosity in learners is fostered.

2. Free creative activity, self-expression, spontaneity and originality are encouraged.

3. Learners are encouraged in divergent thinking and modes of expression.

INDEX

140 Index